PRAISE FOR *ROLLOUT*

"Eighty percent of your EOS results come from rolling out the five foundational tools properly to everyone in your company. This book provides a step-by-step roadmap to help you do exactly that. Marisa and Beth understand both the psychology of change and the real-world challenges of taking EOS to the next level—and they'll show you how to make it happen."

—Gino Wickman
Author of *Traction* & *Shine*, Creator of EOS®

"This is the EOS book I've always dreamed of but never thought to ask for! Every single page is steeped in wisdom, nuance, and compassion for the reader. Outside of Traction, I believe this book will become one of the single most helpful EOS references out there—discussing the full sweep of potential rollout paths, circumstances, and considerations that will genuinely increase clients' confidence in their EOS journey."

—Jeremy Lopatin
Professional EOS Implementer®

"This book is incredibly practical and addresses a critical need for companies running on EOS. Rollout is an area where many leadership teams struggle with what to do, how to do it, and what success looks like. This book guides them through one of the most important processes an EOS company will execute. It serves as both a reference guide and workbook, including helpful tools for effective execution that teams can actually use and remember."

—Mike Gruley
Certified EOS Implementer®

"I am SO excited about this book and can't wait to start using it with my clients! Leadership team alignment is critical to gaining traction, but Rollout is where the magic really starts to happen for companies running on EOS. The practical tools and insights in this book will make all the difference for companies ready to fully embrace EOS and see real transformation in their organizations."

—Jill Young
Expert EOS Implementer™

"ROLLOUT is 'THE' EOS® book I've been waiting for since 2012. After working in over 35 companies that run on EOS, I can confirm that every Rollout is unique and, yes, hard. With *ROLLOUT*, I finally have a clear guidebook that explains why and provides proven tools and methods to navigate the Rollout journey. If you are genuinely ready to 'Take EOS to the Next Level,' you must read this book!"

—Rick Wilson
Integrator, Coach, and Founding Member of the
True Integrator™ Community

"As a multi-location company, this book provided the clear, practical guidance we needed to roll out EOS across all our business units while ensuring we kept the culture we have invested so much time and energy in. Several points of guidance throughout the book helped shape our thinking about what really mattered in our Rollout, and it sharpened and unified our message."

—Scott Longfellow
Integrator at Huyett

"I had implemented EOS once before, but it was challenging to create a clear Rollout plan. This time, with the book in hand, the difference was striking. As a practical guide, it helped us design a comprehensive Rollout plan we could actually follow and gave our team the confidence and clarity we needed."

—Dan Hirst
Integrator at Barrett and Stokely

"If you're serious about unlocking the full power of EOS across your entire organization, this is your blueprint for success. A must-read for every EOS company and EOS Implementer."

—Elizabeth Davis
Certified EOS Implementer

"This is the definitive guide for you to implement the Five Foundational Tools of EOS. It's also your moment of truth. Understand, teach, and embrace these simple tools to maximize the growth of your organization."

—Rene Boer
Author of *How to Be a Great Boss*

ROLLOUT

GET YOUR ENTIRE TEAM RUNNING ON EOS® TO ACHIEVE YOUR VISION

ROLLOUT

GET YOUR ENTIRE TEAM RUNNING ON EOS® TO ACHIEVE YOUR VISION

Marisa Smith & Beth Fahey

EOS
IMPACT

Printed in the United States of America

Published by Igniting Souls
PO Box 43, Powell, OH 43065
IgnitingSouls.com

LCCN: 2025927456
Hardcover ISBN: 978-1-63680-589-4
e-Book ISBN: 978-1-63680-590-0

Available in hardcover, e-book, and audiobook.

Any Internet addresses (websites, blogs, etc.) and telephone numbers printed in this book are offered as a resource. They are not intended in any way to be or imply an endorsement by Igniting Souls, nor does Igniting Souls vouch for the content of these sites and numbers for the life of this book.

Some names and identifying details may have been changed to protect the privacy of individuals.

EOS®, The Entrepreneurial Operating System®, Traction®, and EOS Implementer® are registered trademarks owned by EOS Worldwide, LLC. For a complete list of trademarks owned by EOS Worldwide throughout this book, please visit branding.eosworldwide.com/eos-trademarks/.

The content of this book reflects the author's personal experiences, opinions, and interpretations. The inclusion of any individual, living or deceased, or any organization or entity, is not intended to malign, defame, or harm the reputation of such persons or entities. All statements regarding individuals are solely the author's perspective and do not represent verified facts unless expressly cited to a verifiable source.

The publisher has not independently investigated or confirmed the accuracy of any such references and disclaims all responsibility for them. Nothing in this book should be construed as factual assertions about the character, conduct, or reputation of any individual or entity mentioned. Any resemblance to persons living or dead is purely coincidental unless explicitly stated.

The publisher expressly disclaims liability for any alleged loss, damage, or injury arising from any perceived defamatory content or reliance upon statements within this work. Responsibility for the views, depictions, and representations rests solely with the author.

To the entrepreneurial leaders in the trenches—we see you, we've been you, and we love you for the work you're doing. You've chosen to run your company on EOS. That choice will change lives—your employees, their families, your customers, and people you'll never even meet. Enjoy the journey. It's worth it.

TABLE OF CONTENTS

SUSTAINABILITY

APPENDICES

FOREWORD BY GINO WICKMAN

Many entrepreneurial companies struggle because their precious human energy is spent managing the friction and frustration that exists when everyone in the company is rowing in different directions. The leaders of these companies frequently feel trapped—they're exhausted and have little energy left at the end of the day to move their businesses forward. They're stuck, and they don't know how to break through to the next level.

I created EOS® (the Entrepreneurial Operating System®) to help these leaders regain control of their businesses—to stop feeling stuck and start gaining traction. EOS is, at its core, a system for managing human energy. The EOS Model®, EOS Process®, and EOS Toolbox™ are designed to help you get everyone on the same page with where you're going as a company and how you're going to get there. If you can get all of the human energy in your company going in the same direction, amazing things will happen.

It sounds simple enough, but it's not easy. To get everyone in the company on the same page, you must roll out the vision and EOS beyond the leadership team. Unfortunately, many leadership teams struggle with Rollout because they read *Traction*, start using the tools, get excited about their vision, and then assume everyone else will just get on board.

That assumption is where most rollouts stall, slow down, or fail altogether. Here's what I've learned after watching hundreds of thousands of companies implement EOS: There's a significant difference between understanding the tools at the leadership team level and getting them to work effectively throughout the entire organization.

I started addressing this challenge when Tom Bouwer and I wrote *What the Heck is EOS?* to help employees understand the basics and be more receptive to learning and using EOS, which is working very well.

And now, *Rollout: Get Your Entire Team Running on EOS® to Achieve Your Vision* takes the next step and addresses the core issue: why EOS frequently gets stuck at the leadership team level and stays there, because Rollout requires a different set of skills and strategies than learning and using the tools themselves.

When I learned that Marisa and Beth were writing this book, I knew they were the right people to take this on. As Expert EOS Implementers who have been thought leaders in our community for years, they understand the real-world challenges of implementing EOS throughout an organization. They've tackled these challenges head-on with a thorough, practical approach—giving you the step-by-step roadmap you need to successfully roll out the EOS tools to every single person in your company.

What makes this book unique is that it also digs into the psychology of change and why rollout is inherently challenging. You may understand how to use the EOS tools at the leadership team level, but if you don't know why people resist change and how to work with human nature instead of against it, you're going to struggle. People will be confused. You'll get resistance. Tools will be used inconsistently or abandoned altogether.

The key insight running through this entire book is that successful rollout requires you to take responsibility and become a teacher and coach for your team: providing context, establishing clear expectations, communicating clearly, and consistently demonstrating your commitment to your vision and EOS.

Marisa and Beth wrote this book for anyone responsible for rolling out the EOS Foundational Tools—not just Visionaries. Whether you're an Integrator, Leadership Team member, or mid-manager, *Rollout* will help you drive change and provide the leadership your team needs to transform your business and achieve your vision.

If you're ready to stop hoping your people will figure things out on their own and start systematically rolling out EOS throughout your entire company, this book will show you exactly how to make it happen.

—Gino Wickman
Author of *Traction* & *Shine*, Creator of EOS®

INTRODUCTION

As Expert EOS Implementers, we've helped organizations implement the Entrepreneurial Operating System® (EOS®) and guided leadership teams through every phase of the journey—from initial adoption to company-wide EOS Rollout. In our years of experience as Implementers, we've witnessed both spectacular Rollout successes and painful failures.

When we began collaborating on this book, we quickly discovered we were both lifelong musicians and self-proclaimed choir nerds. That shared background led us to a powerful realization: rolling out EOS in an organization is remarkably similar to teaching a choir a new piece of music.

Picture this: A choir director stands in front of a group of singers, each holding the same piece of sheet music. At first attempt, the result is cacophonous—some singers are in the wrong key, others are behind the beat, and a few seem to be singing an entirely different song. The notes on the page are correct, but the execution is chaotic.

And then something remarkable happens. With patient instruction, consistent practice, and gentle correction, the individual voices begin to blend. The melody emerges. Harmonies lock into place. Eventually, the choir sings with such unity that they barely need to look at the music—they can focus entirely on the conductor's guidance, responding as one to every subtle cue.

Rolling out EOS follows the same pattern. The first time your team hears you talk about your vision and the EOS tools, it may feel confusing and overwhelming. Different people interpret the same concepts differently. Some embrace the changes immediately, while others resist. The "music" of the organization may sound discordant at first.

However, with consistent practice, patient teaching, and deliberate repetition, the concepts begin to take hold. The terminology becomes second nature. The tools start working together as a system. And eventually, your entire organization will know your vision and EOS so well that they'll all be working together in perfect harmony—each person playing their part in service of something much bigger than themselves.

Unfortunately, we've also witnessed organizations where the "choir" never comes together—where EOS tools are implemented inconsistently, team members remain confused about the vision, and the promise of organizational clarity remains frustratingly out of reach. Just as a choir director must ensure that every singer understands not only their individual part but also how it fits into the whole, leaders must help every team member understand not only the EOS tools but also their role in achieving the company's vision.

WHY WE WROTE THIS BOOK

Too many organizations struggle with the gap between the leadership team learning EOS tools and successfully implementing them company-wide. While EOS itself is simple and powerful, the Rollout process—getting every person in your organization to understand, embrace, and consistently use the system—requires careful planning and persistent execution.

Through our work with companies of all sizes and industries, we've identified the most common challenges that derail Rollouts:

- **Inconsistent adoption** across departments and levels of the organization

- **Communication breakdowns** that leave team members confused about the vision and their role

- **Loss of momentum** when initial enthusiasm fades, and old habits resurface

- **Lack of commitment and accountability** of leaders in maintaining EOS disciplines and practices

- **Resistance to change** from team members who don't understand the "why" behind EOS

- **Leadership teams** who understand EOS but struggle to cascade it effectively throughout their organization

More importantly, we've learned what separates successful Rollouts from failed ones. The companies that thrive don't just implement tools and change processes; they create a movement that transforms the culture. They don't just roll out EOS; they bring their vision to life in ways that energize and align every person in the organization.

This book distills those lessons into a practical guide that helps you avoid common pitfalls and accelerate your path to organizational alignment.

WHO THIS BOOK IS FOR

This book speaks directly to leaders who will drive EOS Rollout in their organizations: Visionaries, Integrators, other leadership team members, and next-level leaders (also called Mid-Managers). While your entire company will benefit from the EOS Rollout, this guide is designed for the leaders who will plan, champion, and execute the process. When we use "you" and "your" throughout this book, we're speaking directly to these key leaders who have the responsibility and authority to make Rollout successful.

This book is for four types of leaders and organizations at different stages of their EOS journey:

Companies early in their EOS Journey, working with an EOS Implementer®. You're investing significant time and money in professional guidance. This book will help you maximize that investment by understanding what to expect during Rollout, preparing your team for change, and working most effectively with your Implementer to ensure organization-wide adoption. Think of it as your insider's guide to getting the most out of the EOS Process.

Companies early in their EOS Journey, NOT working with an EOS Implementer. You've decided to implement EOS using *Traction* and other resources, but you're doing it without professional guidance. This book provides the roadmap you need to successfully roll out the system across your entire organization. You'll learn to anticipate challenges, avoid common pitfalls, and maintain momentum throughout the process.

Companies that need a reboot on their Rollout. Your initial EOS implementation started strong but has since stalled or lost momentum. Maybe Level 10 Meetings have become inconsistent, Rocks aren't getting completed, or people have reverted to old habits. This book offers practical strategies for diagnosing what went wrong and relaunching your EOS journey with renewed energy and better execution.

Companies whose understanding of EOS is "stuck" at the leadership team level. You've successfully implemented EOS in the leadership team, but you haven't introduced the vision and/or EOS Tools to other people in the company. You're still solving all of the issues and feel the weight of responsibility for everything on your shoulders. The leadership team is stuck in the day-to-day, and rolling out to the organization seems too big and overwhelming. This book provides the guidance you need to finally take the vision and EOS to the next level.

THE ROLE OF INTERNAL CHAMPIONS

A successful Rollout needs champions—people inside your organization who take ownership of the process and keep it moving forward. While the entire leadership team must be engaged, one person should serve as the primary Rollout Champion, coordinating efforts and maintaining momentum. In our experience, the Integrator often owns this role because Rollout is fundamentally about execution. However, if another member of the leadership team is particularly execution-driven, you might decide it makes more sense for them to own the Rollout Champion role. We'll explore how to identify and develop these champions throughout the book, but it's important to understand from the beginning that Rollout success depends on having the right people in these crucial roles.

A NOTE ABOUT PROFESSIONAL EOS IMPLEMENTERS

Professional EOS Implementers bring valuable experience and objectivity to the Rollout process, helping significantly accelerate your success. They help assess your organization's readiness with an outside perspective, guide you through common pitfalls we've seen hundreds of times before, and hold the leadership team accountable for maintaining EOS disciplines when the pressure mounts. Perhaps most importantly, EOS Implementers are skilled at identifying and addressing team health issues—the interpersonal dynamics, trust gaps, and communication breakdowns that are often the real reason organizations hit the ceiling in the first place.

While determined leadership teams can certainly succeed with self-implementation using the guidance in this book, companies working with a Professional EOS Implementer® typically experience faster adoption, fewer Rollout obstacles, and more sustainable long-term results. Regardless of which path you choose, this book will help you maximize your success by understanding what an excellent Rollout looks like and how to achieve it in your unique organization.

*⚲ **Mastery Tip**: Want to understand what working with a Professional EOS Implementer looks like? Read* Get a Grip *by Gino Wickman and Mike Paton, which follows a leadership team through their complete EOS journey and shows how the tools come together in practice.*

WHAT YOU'LL LEARN

In the pages that follow, you'll discover a systematic four-phase approach to EOS Rollout. Think of these as the natural progression from "We have a vision" to "We're living our vision every single day."

ROLLOUT ROADMAP:

1. **PREPARATION**—Building Your Foundation. Before you can roll out effectively, you need to ensure you're truly ready. This phase helps you assess your organization's readiness for Rollout and identify potential obstacles before they derail your progress. You'll also create a planning framework that you can adapt to your company's unique size, culture, and circumstances—because there's no one-size-fits-all approach to getting everyone rowing in the same direction.

2. **LAUNCH**—Introducing the Vision and EOS. You'll learn communication strategies that build excitement rather than resistance around change, along with proven methods for creating momentum rather than confusion. The goal isn't just to share information—it's to invite everyone into a shared future that they want to help create.

3. **INTEGRATION**—Taking EOS Deeper. Launch creates awareness, but Integration creates mastery. This phase focuses on department-by-department Rollout techniques that ensure consistency while respecting team differences, as well as methods for bringing your vision to life in daily operations, not just in quarterly meetings. This is where EOS stops being something you talk about and starts being how you actually operate.

4. **SUSTAINABILITY**—Running on EOS... forever. You'll learn strategies to maintain momentum amid inevitable challenges and setbacks. This is where you shift from implementing EOS to simply running on it—making it your permanent operating system rather than a temporary improvement program.

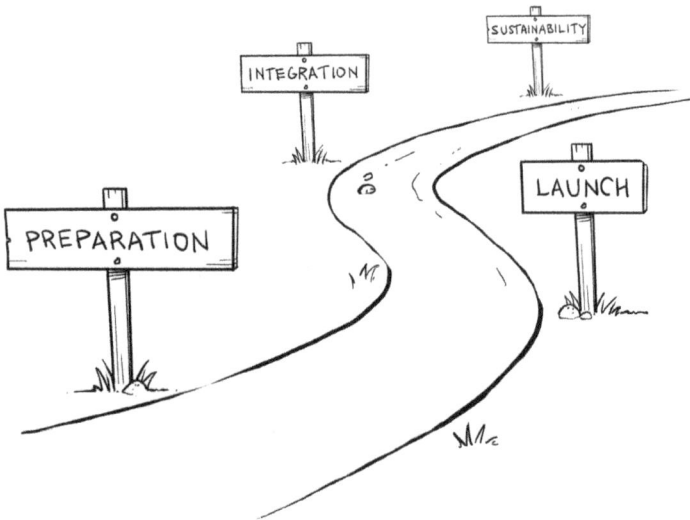

Within each phase, you'll learn specific strategies for creating lasting change by building accountability systems and maintaining EOS discipline forever. This guide will help you successfully plan and execute your Rollout so your entire team can work together with the precision and harmony of a world-class choir.

HOW TO GET THE MOST FROM THIS BOOK

Before you dive in, here are a few suggestions to maximize your success.

Read with the entire leadership team. While one person can read this book and drive Rollout, the best results come when the entire leadership team understands and commits to the process together.

Focus on progress, not perfection. You'll never feel 100 percent ready for Rollout. Your first attempts at Rollout won't be flawless. That's not only okay—it's expected. What matters is consistent effort and continuous improvement.

Use this book as a reference. Don't let it gather dust on your bookshelf. Refer back to relevant chapters as new challenges arise or as you move to different phases of your Rollout.

Learning without reflection is forgotten. Use the Reflection Questions at the end of the chapters to clarify your thinking and align the leadership team to create a successful Rollout Plan.

Use the Chapter Summaries as reference guides. Each chapter ends with a summary that distills the key concepts and main takeaways. These aren't just review material—they're quick reference guides you can return to throughout your Rollout to refresh your understanding or share key points with your team.

Use the practical tools in the appendices. This book includes practical tools designed to support your Rollout:

- Rollout Tracker: Use this tool to establish your baseline and keep track of your progress during your Rollout journey

- The Organizational Checkup: Assess your organization's strength in the Six Key Components® of the EOS Model to see how well your rollout is working

- Rollout Reflection Guide: A comprehensive planning tool to use throughout the Rollout process

- Rollout Troubleshooting Guide: Solutions for the ten most common Rollout challenges

*Look for the ✂ **Rollout Tool** callouts throughout each chapter that direct you to these resources at the most relevant moments.*

Ready to begin? Let's start making beautiful music together...

SETTING THE STAGE

1

THE JOURNEY TO 100% STRONG

*If you can get all of the people in a company rowing in the
same direction, you can dominate in any industry,
against any competition, at any time.*

—Patrick Lencioni

When you decided to implement the Entrepreneurial
Operating System, you embarked on a journey to become
100 percent strong in the Six Key Components of the
EOS Model: Vision, People, Data, Issues, Process, and Traction®.

EOS is based on a simple but powerful premise: all of the
issues you're experiencing in your business are symptoms of
weakness in one of these Six Key Components. By implementing and mastering EOS tools and disciplines, you'll strengthen
these components and solve your issues—for good.

When you're 100 percent strong, it should look something like this:

- **Vision:** Everyone in the company is crystal clear on where you're going as a company and how you're going to get there.
- **People:** All of the people in your company share your core values, and GWC® (Get, Want, and have the Capacity to execute) their seats.
- **Data:** You have an absolute pulse on your business, with Scorecards in place at the Company and Departmental Level, and every person in the company having at least one number they're accountable for.
- **Issues:** Your culture is open, honest, and transparent, and everyone in the company is comfortable bringing up issues and has a shared methodology to IDS® (Identify, Discuss, and Solve) the root issue.

- **Process:** Your core processes are documented and simplified, and you consistently train, manage, and measure to ensure they are FBA (Followed By All).
- **Traction:** Everyone in the organization has at least one Rock per quarter and is engaged in a meeting pulse to drive accountability.

Of course, achieving 100 percent strong in all Six Key Components is utopia—a perfect state that's worth striving for but rarely achieved. In reality, if you can get into the 80+ percent range and maintain it consistently, that's a pretty great company to own and be a part of.

At 80+ percent strong, you'll experience what could be described as "organizational flow"—that state where everything feels effortless because all the pieces are working together. Decisions get made quickly because everyone understands the vision. Problems get solved efficiently because they're identified early and addressed systematically. People perform at their best because they're clear on expectations and accountable for results.

CHANGE STARTS AT THE TOP

The fastest and most efficient way to achieve 80+ percent strong is to follow the EOS Process, which is designed to help you gain traction as efficiently and effectively as possible.

One of the refrains we repeat in the EOS Community is, "As goes the leadership team, so goes the rest of the organization." This isn't just a catchy phrase—it's how change is implemented most effectively in entrepreneurial organizations.

Think about it: If the leadership team can't consistently run effective meetings, how can you expect your departments to do so? If the leaders aren't aligned on the vision, how can you expect employees to be? If the leadership team doesn't demonstrate accountability with Rocks and Measurables, why would anyone else?

This is why the EOS Process focuses initially on aligning the leadership team—the three to seven people at the helm of the organization who are responsible for key functional areas such as Sales, Marketing, Operations, Finance, and HR. During the first three sessions (Focus Day®, Vision Building® Day 1, and Vision Building Day 2), this team works intensively to master the EOS Foundational Tools while clarifying the organization's vision and structure.

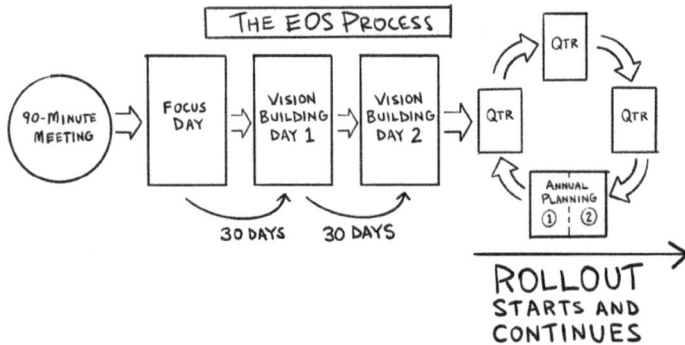

As you can see from the EOS Process graphic, these initial sessions are spaced about 30 days apart. This timing is intentional—it gives the leadership team time to absorb new concepts, practice new behaviors, and begin seeing results before adding the next layer of complexity.

At first, the tools may feel foreign, and the new behaviors may feel uncomfortable. Some leaders will embrace the changes immediately, while others may need more time to see the value. Level 10 Meetings might feel forced, Rock-setting may seem arbitrary, and accountability conversations could create tension.

And then, with consistent practice and patience, something remarkable happens. The tools begin to work together as a system. The leadership team starts functioning as a true team rather than a collection of individual contributors. Trust builds, communication improves, and results follow.

If you're working with a Professional EOS Implementer, they will likely introduce the concept of Rollout at Vision Building Day 2, or when your leadership team is ready to consider sharing your vision and EOS with the rest of the organization. Once the leadership team has done the hard work of getting aligned themselves, they must prepare to lead others through the same transformation.

You're on your way to strengthening the Six Key Components, but there's more work to be done.

GETTING TO THE NEXT LEVEL

You started using EOS because you wanted more from your business. You may have felt stuck or frustrated, hitting a ceiling that you couldn't seem to break through. You saw EOS as a way to reach the next level—more profit, the right people, improved control, enhanced growth, or simply a more fulfilling work experience.

The reality is that getting to the next level requires real change in how you and your team operate, think, and behave. To achieve 80+ percent strength in all Six Key Components, you must take EOS beyond the leadership team and get everyone in your organization to understand the concepts, use the tools, and embrace the vision.

This sounds simple, but as anyone who has tried to implement change knows, it's rarely easy.

Many leaders underestimate the human side of change. They focus on the logical, rational aspects (the tools, processes, and systems) while neglecting the emotional and psychological aspects (fear, resistance, and ingrained habits).

If you've ever tried to roll out a new software system, implement a new process, or even change the brand of coffee in the office, you already know that humans don't always embrace change—even when the promised result is an improvement over the current state. Sometimes it can feel like most of your team's energy goes into resisting change rather than implementing it.

This resistance isn't defiance or stubbornness (usually). It's biology. Our brains are literally wired to prefer familiar patterns over new ones, even when the new patterns would serve us better. Understanding this reality is the first step toward successfully navigating it.

ALIGNING HUMAN ENERGY

The good news is that EOS is a system for managing human energy. Before implementing EOS, the human energy in most organizations is unfocused, disorganized, or even downright chaotic. Without clear direction and prioritization, these teams waste precious time and energy working at cross-purposes or running around in circles.

Picture a team of people trying to move a large boulder. Without coordination, they push in different directions, work at different times, and use different techniques. Despite everyone's best efforts, the boulder barely moves, and everyone ends up exhausted and frustrated.

ALIGNING HUMAN ENERGY

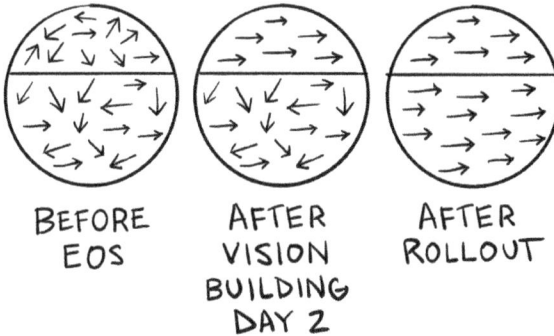

BEFORE   AFTER   AFTER
EOS   VISION   ROLLOUT
                BUILDING
                DAY 2

When you began implementing EOS, the leadership team invested considerable time together—three full days over 60–90 days—to align on the right organizational structure and create clarity around your vision. By the end of Vision Building Day 2, the leadership team's energy should be aligned and pointing in the same direction.

Here's the key insight: while the leadership team has achieved alignment, the rest of the organization hasn't yet made this journey. You have one small group pushing the boulder in perfect coordination while everyone else is still pushing in different directions.

The goal of Rollout is to align and focus ALL of the human energy in your organization on achieving a shared vision of success. When this happens, the boulder doesn't just move—it gains momentum and becomes easier to push over time.

This transformation of human energy is what creates the breakthrough results that EOS companies experience. Instead of energy being wasted on internal friction, competing priorities, and unclear direction, it all flows toward achieving the vision.

TWO ESSENTIAL ROLLOUT TOOLS

To guide your way on this journey, you need to track two things: what you've implemented and whether it's actually working. Two tools will help you measure your progress:

- **The Rollout Tracker** answers the question: *What have we implemented?* It tracks your progress through the four phases of Rollout (Preparation, Launch, Integration, and Sustainability), showing you what's complete and what still needs to be done.

- **The Organizational Checkup** answers: *Is it working?* It measures the strength of your organization in relation to the Six Key Components of the EOS Model (Vision, People, Data, Issues, Process, and Traction) and helps you see the progress you are making on your journey to 100 percent strong.

Throughout this book, we'll reference both tools. The Rollout Tracker tells you what you've implemented. The Organizational Checkup tells you if it's working. You need both to gauge real progress.

Complete both assessments now, before you read another page. Spend a few minutes completing them to establish your baseline. You'll return to both tools multiple times throughout your Rollout journey, watching your progress quarter by quarter.

ROLLOUT TRACKER

Answer YES or NO based on where you honestly are today. Don't judge yourself—most organizations start with mostly "NO" answers—that's normal. Use these to identify what needs attention next in your Rollout Plan. Return to the assessment at the end of each phase to track progress.

- **OPTION A:** Download a printable version at **RolloutBook.com**
- **OPTION B:** Use the 1-page tool in Appendix A of this book

ROLLOUT TRACKER:

GET YOUR ENTIRE TEAM RUNNING ON EOS

Rollout equips your entire team with the tools they need to help you achieve your vision. Fully implementing EOS requires leadership team mastery, a clear plan, and commitment to make it stick. Every organization is different, so develop a Rollout plan that's right for you.

HOW TO USE THIS TRACKER:

- Establish Your Baseline: Complete this assessment before beginning your Rollout to see where you are today
- Update Regularly: Return to it periodically to measure progress
- Identify Next Steps: Use your "NO" answers to identify what needs attention next

ANSWER YES OR NO TO EACH ITEM BELOW BASED ON WHERE YOU ARE TODAY:

1. PREPARATION: THE LEADERSHIP TEAM IS READY FOR ROLLOUT ☐YES ☐NO

- Align and get ready to communicate the 5 EOS Foundational Tools™ (V/TO®, The Accountability Chart®, Rocks, The Meeting Pulse®, and Scorecard)
- Create Rollout Plan (Timeline, Roles & Responsibilities, Communication, etc.)

2. LAUNCH: THE LEADERSHIP TEAM HAS INTRODUCED THE VISION AND EOS ☐YES ☐NO

- Introduce your EOS Foundational Tools (context + content) to the organization
  - V/TO: Deliver the Core Values Speech and review each section
  - The Accountability Chart: Share the structure, functions, and roles
  - Rocks: Share your Company Rocks for the next quarter
  - The Meeting Pulse: Explain Level 10 Meetings, Quarterlies, and Annuals
  - Scorecard: Explain the importance of data and measurables
- Hand out a copy of *What the Heck is EOS?* to everyone
- Plan your next Quarterly State of the Company meeting to share:
  - Where we've been
  - Where we are
  - Where we're going

3. INTEGRATION: EOS TOOLS AND DISCIPLINES ARE FULLY INTEGRATED COMPANY-WIDE ☐YES ☐NO

- Departments:
  - Meet regularly using the Level 10 Meeting Agenda
  - Meet quarterly to review the Company V/TO and Departmental Plan, set Departmental and Individual Rocks, and solve issues
  - Meet annually to review the Company V/TO, update the Departmental Plan (Goals and Rocks), and solve issues
- Core Processes are documented, simplified, and Followed by All (FBA)
- Everyone has at least one number they are accountable for keeping on track
- Leaders and Managers:
  - Use Core Values to hire, fire, review, reward, and recognize
  - Have read *How to Be a Great Boss* and understand LMA
  - Are answering YES to the Leadership & Management Self-Assessments
  - Are holding Quarterly Conversations with direct reports

4. SUSTAINABILITY: THE LEADERSHIP TEAM IS COMMITTED TO RUNNING ON EOS...FOREVER ☐YES ☐NO

- Deliver a State of the Company every quarter
- Achieve and maintain 80%+ on the Organizational Checkup®
  - Annually as a Leadership Team
  - Annually (or quarterly, if preferred) as an entire organization
- Complete 80%+ of Goals every year
- Complete 80%+ of Rocks every quarter
- Complete 90%+ of To-Dos weekly

ORGANIZATIONAL CHECKUP®

Complete this as a leadership team to measure the strength of your organization across the Six Key Components of the EOS Model.

- **Option A:** Complete the assessment online at **OrganizationalCheckup.com** for automatic scoring and comprehensive reporting
- **Option B:** Use the 2-page Organizational Checkup in your Leadership Team Manual or in Appendix B.

▌ ORGANIZATIONAL CHECKUP®

FOR EACH STATEMENT BELOW, RANK YOUR BUSINESS ON A SCALE OF 1 TO 5 WHERE 1 IS WEAK AND 5 IS STRONG.

	1	2	3	4	5
1. We have a clear vision in writing that has been properly communicated and is shared by everyone in the company.	☐	☐	☐	☐	☐
2. Our Core Values are clear, and we hire, fire, review, reward, and recognize around them.	☐	☐	☐	☐	☐
3. Our Core Focus (core business) is clear, and we keep our people, systems, and processes aligned and focused on it.	☐	☐	☐	☐	☐
4. Our 10-Year Target (big, long-range business goal) is clear, communicated regularly, and is shared by all.	☐	☐	☐	☐	☐
5. Our target market (definition of our ideal customer) is clear, and all of our marketing and sales efforts are focused on it.	☐	☐	☐	☐	☐
6. Our 3 Uniques (differentiators) are clear, and all of our marketing and sales efforts communicate them.	☐	☐	☐	☐	☐
7. We have a proven process for doing business with our customers. It has been named and visually illustrated, and all of our salespeople use it.	☐	☐	☐	☐	☐
8. All of the people in our organization are the "right people" (they fit our culture and share our Core Values).	☐	☐	☐	☐	☐
9. Our Accountability Chart (organizational chart that includes roles/responsibilities) is clear, complete, and constantly updated.	☐	☐	☐	☐	☐
10. Everyone is in the "right seat" (they "get it, want it, and have the capacity to do their jobs well").	☐	☐	☐	☐	☐
11. Our leadership team is open and honest and demonstrates a high level of trust.	☐	☐	☐	☐	☐
12. Everyone has Rocks (1 to 7 priorities per quarter) and is focused on them.	☐	☐	☐	☐	☐

ORGANIZATIONAL CHECKUP

	1	2	3	4	5
13. Everyone is engaged in a regular Meeting Pulse (weekly, quarterly, annually).	☐	☐	☐	☐	☐
14. All meetings are on the same day and at the same time, have the same agenda, start on time, and end on time.	☐	☐	☐	☐	☐
15. All teams clearly identify, discuss, and solve issues for the long-term greater good of the company.	☐	☐	☐	☐	☐
16. Our Core Processes are documented, simplified, and Followed By All to consistently produce the results we want.	☐	☐	☐	☐	☐
17. We have systems for receiving regular feedback from customers and employees, so we always know their level of satisfaction.	☐	☐	☐	☐	☐
18. A Scorecard(s) for tracking weekly metrics/measurables is in place to consistently predict that we are on track to achieve the results we want.	☐	☐	☐	☐	☐
19. Everyone in the organization has at least one number they are accountable for keeping on track each week.	☐	☐	☐	☐	☐
20. We have a budget and are monitoring it regularly (e.g., monthly or quarterly).	☐	☐	☐	☐	☐
Total number of each ranking	☐	☐	☐	☐	☐
	x1	x2	x3	x4	x5
Multiply by the number above	☐	☐	☐	☐	☐

Add all five numbers to determine the percentage score that reflects the current state of your company: ☐ %

WHY SOME TEAMS HESITATE

After completing these assessments, you might be feeling a mix of emotions. Perhaps you're excited about the potential but also anxious about the reality of what lies ahead. Many leadership teams pause at this threshold for various reasons:

- **Fear of how team members will react** to change and new expectations
- **Desire to wait until the vision is "perfect"** before sharing it
- **Uncertainty about their own knowledge** if they can't answer every question
- **Concern about creating more work** for an already busy organization
- **Lack of alignment or full commitment** to their vision and/or the value of rolling out EOS beyond the leadership team
- **Not knowing where to start** or how to manage the process

While these concerns are understandable, delaying Rollout actually makes the problem worse. The longer you wait to begin aligning human energy throughout your organization, the longer it will take to achieve the vision. Meanwhile, the misaligned energy continues to create inefficiency, frustration, and missed opportunities.

Here's the fundamental truth that drives successful Rollout:

To achieve your vision, it must be Shared By All.
To get your vision Shared By All, you must roll out EOS.

This brings us to the central question: What the heck does it mean to roll out EOS?

CHAPTER 1 SUMMARY

EOS is designed to strengthen the Six Key Components of your organization, taking you on a journey toward 100 percent strong in Vision, People, Data, Issues, Process, and Traction. While 100 percent represents utopia, achieving 80+ percent strength creates "organizational flow" where everything feels effortless because all pieces work together harmoniously.

- **Change must start with the leadership team alignment** before cascading throughout the organization. Just as you can't expect departments to run effective meetings if the leadership team can't, organizational transformation begins at the top and flows down systematically. The fastest path to 80+ percent strong is following the EOS Process, which focuses initially on aligning the leadership team through intensive work on mastering the EOS Foundational Tools.

- **The goal of Rollout is to align human energy** throughout your entire organization toward achieving a shared vision. Without EOS, human energy in most organizations is scattered, disorganized, or chaotic—like people pushing a boulder in different directions. When everyone's energy becomes aligned through Rollout, the boulder doesn't just move—it gains momentum and becomes easier to push over time.

- To achieve your vision, it must be **Shared By All**, and to get your vision Shared By All, you must roll out EOS throughout your organization.

The journey to aligning human energy throughout your organization begins with understanding exactly what you're asking people to embrace. You've learned that EOS can transform scattered energy into focused momentum, but what does that transformation actually look like in practice?

What's Next: In Chapter 2, we'll define exactly what Rollout means, why it's a journey rather than an event, and why it represents a revolutionary change in how your organization operates.

REFLECTION QUESTIONS

1. **Human Energy Assessment**: Looking at our current state, is our human energy scattered in different directions, or is it mostly aligned? What would need to change to get everyone "pushing the boulder" in the same direction?

2. **Tool Readiness**: After completing the Rollout Tracker and Organizational Checkup, what surprised us most about where we are? What gaps feel most urgent to address?

2

WHAT THE HECK IS ROLLOUT?

80 percent of the battle is rolling out the
EOS Foundational Tools from top to bottom.

—Gino Wickman

I n a nutshell, **Rollout is how you equip your entire team with the EOS tools they need to help you turn your vision into reality.**

Think of Rollout as teaching your organizational choir to sing a complex piece of music. You can't just hand out sheet music and expect beautiful harmony. You need to teach each section their part, help them understand how their part fits with others, practice together until the music becomes natural, and develop the discipline to perform consistently—even when the choir director isn't standing right there.

While the EOS Toolbox includes more than 20 tools, Rollout primarily focuses on helping everyone in the organization understand and master the five **EOS Foundational Tools**.

1. Vision/Traction Organizer® (V/TO®)
2. The Accountability Chart®
3. Rocks
4. The Meeting Pulse®
5. Scorecard

Depending on your organization's size, Rollout typically flows one tier or team at a time—from the leadership team to mid-managers (department heads and key managers who report to leadership), then to their individual teams or departments. In future chapters, we'll explore what this looks like in practice. Once these five Foundational Tools are working well throughout the organization, you may choose to introduce additional EOS tools and disciplines (ex., The People Analyzer®, Organizational Checkup, and more than 20 others) to further strengthen the Six Key Components.

When these five Foundational Tools are fully implemented throughout your organization, the transformation is remarkable. Your team will operate with a shared vision, eliminating the confusion that comes from everyone working from different playbooks. Instead of crisis-driven priorities and random meetings, you'll see disciplined focus, with competing demands replaced by clear quarterly Rocks. Communication becomes precise through shared language, while accountability shifts from optional to expected as role confusion gets replaced with measurable standards.

For your organization to be 80 percent or stronger in the Six Key Components of EOS, everyone must understand and use these tools. Notice we said "understand and use," not "perfectly execute." Just as choir members don't need to be professional musicians to contribute to beautiful music, your team members don't need to be EOS experts to help achieve your vision.

The goal is building organizational capability, not individual perfection.

Remember: The purpose of having everyone use these EOS tools isn't merely to "check a box" and claim you're running on EOS. Instead, it's about leveraging EOS to achieve your vision more efficiently and effectively. The tools are a means to an end, not the end itself.

ROLLOUT IS A JOURNEY, NOT AN EVENT

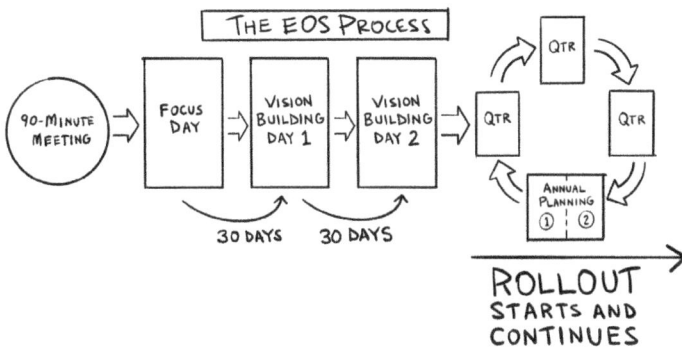

Rollout typically starts after Vision Building Day 2, once the leadership team is aligned on the Vision for the company and ready to share it with the rest of the organization.

One of the biggest misconceptions about EOS Rollout is treating it like a one-time event. Many leaders reach Vision Building Day 2 and think, "Whew! The hard part is over. Our leadership team is aligned on the vision, we have a clear organizational structure, we know how to set Rocks, we're running Level 10 Meetings, and our Scorecard is starting to work. Now we just need to roll this out to everyone else. Let's schedule a meeting for next week and get it done!"

This thinking isn't just flawed—it's dangerous to your Rollout's success.

Consider your own EOS learning experience:

- Did you master Level 10 Meetings right away?
- Did your Scorecard become immediately meaningful after tracking numbers for one week?
- Did you complete 80 percent or more of your Rocks in your first quarter?
- Did you feel completely confident with IDS after your first few attempts?

Of course not. Learning EOS was a process that required time, repetition, refinement, and patience. You had setbacks, moments of confusion, and probably a few meetings that made you wonder if this whole EOS thing was really going to work.

You stuck with it because you started seeing results. Small wins built confidence. Gradual improvements created momentum. And eventually, the tools became second nature—so natural that you can't imagine running your business any other way.

The same journey awaits every person and every team in your organization.

REAL-WORLD EXAMPLE: THE "ONE AND DONE" DISASTER

We know one founder who was excited to share the company's new vision after completing Vision Building Day 2. Against his EOS Implementer's advice, he scheduled a single two-hour all-hands meeting to "roll out EOS to everyone."

He presented the entire V/TO in 45 minutes, walked through The Accountability Chart in 15 minutes, explained Rocks in 10 minutes, and briefly mentioned Level 10 Meetings and Scorecards. He ended with, "Any questions? Great! Let's start implementing these tools immediately."

The results were predictably disastrous:

- Department leaders felt overwhelmed and didn't know where to start
- Employees were confused about what was expected of them
- Three months later, the only evidence of EOS was a few posters on the conference room wall

The founder later admitted, "I thought I was being efficient, but I was actually being lazy. I wanted Rollout to be as simple as giving a presentation, but real change takes much more work."

This company eventually succeeded with EOS, but only after acknowledging that Rollout is a journey requiring patience, repetition, and sustained effort.

Remember, the journey to 80+ percent strong is also a journey to becoming your best—as a leadership team and as an organization. While you may decide to schedule an event to launch your Rollout and introduce the vision and EOS to your team, it will take time, repetition, and patience to get everyone in the company to start rowing in the same direction.

Every organization is unique, every journey is unique, and every Rollout is unique. Depending on the size and complexity of your company, it can take anywhere from a few months to several years to fully roll out the vision and EOS to your entire organization. Enjoy the journey!

ROLLOUT IS REVOLUTIONARY

If you're working with a Professional EOS Implementer, you learned about the concept of "hitting the ceiling" in your Focus Day session—the feeling of being stuck or frustrated, knowing that you want to reach the next level, but not knowing how to get there. Most leaders start to implement EOS because they are experiencing one or more of these five frustrations.

1. **Lack of control**: Your business is running you instead of you running it. You're constantly reacting to problems rather than steering the direction of your company.

2. **People**: Your team, customers, and partners aren't aligned. Expectations are unclear, follow-through is inconsistent, and everyone seems to be working from different playbooks.

3. **Profit**: Your bottom line isn't where it needs to be. Despite all your efforts, the numbers don't reflect the success you're working toward.

4. **Hitting the ceiling**: You've plateaued and can't seem to push through to the next level. The strategies that got you here aren't taking you there, and you're not sure what moves to make.

5. **Nothing's working**: You've tried multiple solutions and systems, but nothing has created lasting change. Your team has become skeptical of new approaches, and you're stuck without real momentum.

Hitting the ceiling is inevitable as companies grow. As Gino Wickman explains in *Traction*, "Reaching the natural limits of your existing resources is a by-product of growth, and a company continually needs to adjust its existing state if it hopes to expand through the next ceiling."[1] If they don't figure out how to break through, they will either flatline or fail.

Breaking through the ceiling requires a period of **revolution**—challenging the status quo and establishing new ways of operating to reach the next level. This isn't gradual evolution; it's transformation.

By implementing EOS, you started a revolution with the potential to transform your organization and propel you forward. While this sounds exciting, revolutions aren't comfortable. They challenge existing power structures, disrupt established routines, and require people to develop new skills and mindsets to continue to evolve and grow.

This revolutionary change process naturally creates the specific organizational capabilities that help you break through the ceiling. As people learn to use the EOS tools consistently, several fundamental shifts occur that directly address the frustrations that brought you to EOS in the first place.

- **Shared Vision** emerges as everyone begins to understand where you're going and how you'll get there—from the high-level, long-term strategy to the tactical goals and priorities you need to execute to achieve it. When decisions need to be made, your team will naturally ask, "Does this align with our vision?" rather than pursuing every opportunity that comes along, directly addressing the lack of control that kept you reactive instead of strategic.

- **Shared Language** develops as your company establishes a common vocabulary that eliminates confusion and creates precision in communication. Terms like Core Values, Rocks, IDS, and GWC become part of your everyday language, allowing your team to communicate complex ideas quickly and clearly. This common language extends beyond EOS terminology to include clarity around your internal processes, systems, and decision-making criteria, ensuring everyone operates from the same understanding of how work gets done—solving the people alignment issues that lead to inconsistent follow-through.

- **Discipline and Focus** replace the scattered energy that kept you hitting the ceiling. Instead of random meetings and crisis-driven priorities, your organization will operate in a disciplined meeting pulse. Competing priorities will get replaced with clear Rocks, enabling your team to avoid distractions and stay focused on what matters most—directly targeting the "nothing's working" frustration by creating a systematic approach to execution.

- **Clear Expectations** transform accountability from optional to expected, replacing role confusion with measurable standards. Performance that was once acceptable may no longer be sufficient as unclear expectations get replaced with specific, trackable outcomes that drive the profit improvements you've been seeking.

- **Healthy and Cohesive Team** dynamics emerge as your team learns to tackle difficult issues head-on instead of letting them fester, using a shared problem-solving approach that builds trust through consistent follow-through.

The energy previously wasted on workplace drama gets redirected toward achieving a shared vision, creating a culture where people actually enjoy working together to solve problems.

This naturally triggers that uncomfortable period between the old way of doing things and the new way, when people feel uncertain, anxious, or resistant. Understanding that EOS Rollout is revolutionary helps you prepare for this discomfort rather than being surprised by it. You can anticipate resistance, plan for confusion, and maintain patience when progress feels slow.

Most importantly, you can help your team understand that the temporary discomfort of change is the price of a breakthrough. Just as a butterfly must struggle to emerge from its chrysalis (and that struggle is what develops the strength to fly), your organization must work through the challenges of Rollout to develop the capabilities that will carry you to the next level.

Unfortunately, most human beings are not naturally wired to embrace revolutionary change, even when it's clearly in their best interest. This brings us to a crucial question: Why is Rollout so hard?

CHAPTER 2 SUMMARY

Rollout is how you equip your entire team with the EOS Foundational Tools they need to help turn the vision into reality. These five tools—V/TO, The Accountability Chart, Rocks, The Meeting Pulse, and Scorecard—must be understood and used by everyone for your organization to achieve 80+ percent strength in the Six Key Components. When fully implemented, these tools create a shared vision, shared language, discipline and focus, clear expectations, and healthy team dynamics.

- **Rollout is a journey, not an event.** Just as learning EOS required time, repetition, and patience for the leadership team, every person in your organization needs the same gradual process to master these concepts.

- **Rollout is revolutionary.** Rollout fundamentally transforms how your organization operates by directly addressing the frustrations that brought you to EOS—lack of control, people alignment issues, profit challenges, hitting the ceiling, and systems that weren't working. This revolutionary change creates shared vision, shared language, discipline and focus, clear expectations, and healthy team dynamics. This level of transformation naturally triggers uncertainty and resistance, but understanding this helps you prepare strategically rather than being surprised by predictable human reactions.

- **The temporary discomfort of revolutionary change is the price of breakthrough results.** Like a butterfly struggling to emerge from its chrysalis, your organization must work through Rollout challenges to develop the capabilities that will carry you to the next level.

Now that you understand that Rollout is a revolutionary journey of transformation, you might be wondering why so many well-intentioned change efforts fail despite having good systems and committed leaders. The answer lies in understanding the fundamental human challenges that make organizational change inherently difficult. Before you can design an effective Rollout strategy, you need to understand the psychological and behavioral obstacles you'll face—not so you can avoid them, but so you can navigate them skillfully.

What's Next: In Chapter 3, we'll explore why Rollout is inherently challenging by examining the psychological and behavioral obstacles you'll face—and how to navigate them successfully.

REFLECTION QUESTIONS

1. **Revolutionary Change Mindset**: How comfortable is our organization with the kind of fundamental change that Rollout represents? What past change initiatives can we learn from—both successes and failures?

2. **Journey vs. Event Reality**: How will we remind ourselves to stay patient with the Rollout process? Are we prepared for this to be a journey rather than an event?

3. **Success Visualization**: Looking at the five outcomes of successful Rollout (shared vision, shared language, discipline and focus, clear expectations, healthy team dynamics), which of these would have the biggest impact on our current frustrations?

3

WHY ROLLOUT IS HARD

All change may not be progress,
but all progress is the result of change.

—John Wooden

You've experienced the power of EOS firsthand. The leadership team has embraced new tools, adopted fresh perspectives, and started seeing real results. You understand how Level 10 Meetings work, how Rocks drive accountability, and how Scorecards help you predict more effectively. So why does the prospect of rolling these same tools out to your entire organization feel so daunting?

The truth is: organizational EOS Rollout is where many well-intentioned change efforts stumble. It's not because EOS doesn't work—hundreds of thousands of companies prove it does. The challenge lies in the fundamental nature of human psychology and behavior.

Your organization is filled with people whose brains work in predictable ways, which is why EOS principles are so effective in the first place. Those same brains, however, are also wired to follow established patterns, resist change, and maintain comfortable routines.

Understanding why EOS Rollout is inherently difficult will help you approach it with the right expectations, strategies, and mindset. This chapter explores the three core challenges you'll face and provides frameworks for navigating them successfully.

REWIRING HUMAN BRAINS

When employees seem to resist your Rollout efforts, they're usually not plotting against you by the water cooler or deliberately undermining your leadership. More often, they're simply wrestling with a basic fact of human biology: changing how we think and behave requires rewiring billions of neural connections that have been operating the same way for years or even decades.

To appreciate the magnitude of this challenge, consider that your brain contains roughly 86 billion neurons connected by trillions of synapses. Every time you learn something new or change a behavior, you're literally creating new neural pathways while weakening old ones. This process requires significant mental energy and feels uncomfortable—which is why your brain often prefers the familiar path of least resistance.

BELIEFS SHAPE REALITY

Your team consists of individuals with deeply held beliefs about leadership, accountability, meetings, and business operations. These beliefs didn't form overnight—they've been reinforced through years of experience in your organization and others. The EOS Model, Process, and Toolbox essentially walk up to these well-established beliefs and say, "Hey, maybe there's a better way to think about this stuff."

For example, consider what your employees might believe about meetings:

- "Meetings are mostly a waste of time where nothing gets decided."
- "The loudest person in the room usually gets their way."
- "We'll discuss the same issues repeatedly without ever solving them."
- "Meetings always run long and prevent me from doing real work."

These beliefs aren't necessarily wrong based on their past experience. Still, they create powerful mental filters that interpret new information through the lens of old assumptions.

When you introduce Level 10 Meetings, you're asking people to change their existing beliefs and embrace the belief that meetings can be productive, focused, and valuable.

This isn't just a philosophical shift—it's also a biological shift. Creating new neural pathways takes real mental effort, while old patterns let your brain cruise on autopilot. Your employees' initial skepticism often reflects their brains saying, "We've tried meeting improvements before, and they didn't stick. Why should this be different?"

THE POWER OF REPETITION AND TIME

Human brains are sophisticated pattern recognition systems that need to encounter information multiple times before accepting it as important. During your Focus Day, you learned about becoming "good parents" to your employees—establishing a handful of clear rules, repeating yourself often, and walking the talk consistently.

We emphasize repeating messages at least seven times—not because seven has magical powers, but because it usually takes that much repetition before people think, "Okay, maybe they're serious about this." This isn't arbitrary—it reflects how human memory and learning actually work.

Equally important is spacing this repetition over time. Hearing something ten times in ten minutes won't create the same impact as encountering it ten times across several weeks. This spaced repetition is essential for forming new neural pathways and genuinely rewiring how people think.

One CEO told us, "I couldn't understand why my smartest people kept asking the same questions about our vision week after week. Then I realized—they weren't being difficult, their brains were literally rewiring to think differently about our business."

YOUR OWN EOS LEARNING JOURNEY

Think back to your own experience with EOS. What beliefs about leadership and business did you hold when you first walked into your Focus Day? Did your perspective shift immediately upon learning about the Five Leadership Abilities (Simplify, Delegate, Predict, Systemize, and Structure), or did it take a few weeks of practice before you truly understood these concepts?

Most leaders find they feel significantly more comfortable with EOS concepts by Vision Building Day 2 than they did initially—not through magic, but through carefully spaced repetition built into the EOS Process.

Now consider that your team is about to embark on the same learning journey you experienced. They'll need the same patience, repetition, and time to develop neural pathways that support EOS thinking.

THE NEUROSCIENCE OF RESISTANCE

Ever wonder why smart people sometimes resist obviously good ideas? It's because their brains are doing exactly what brains are supposed to do—protecting them from perceived threats. When you present information that challenges how someone thinks the world works, their brain can literally go into defense mode, releasing stress hormones that make it harder to think logically about the benefits.

This means that when you present your V/TO or explain new accountability expectations, some people's brains may perceive this as a threat to their existing understanding of how the world works. Their resistance isn't a character defect; it's a predictable biological response.

Understanding this response allows you to work with human psychology rather than against it.

- **Start with why** to engage the brain's natural curiosity before introducing new concepts.

- **Use stories and examples** to help people visualize success rather than focusing on what needs to change.

- **Celebrate small wins** to reinforce new neural pathways with positive emotions.

- **Be patient with the learning curve** while maintaining consistency in your message.

BREAKING COMFORTABLE HABITS

Understanding new concepts intellectually is only half the battle. The greater challenge lies in changing behavior—how people actually act in meetings, handle accountability, approach their work, and interact with colleagues.

Changing behavior is like asking someone to learn a new dance while the music is still playing. Even when they understand the steps intellectually, executing them smoothly requires practice, muscle memory, and the willingness to feel awkward during the learning process.

DEFAULTING TO FAMILIAR PATTERNS

Humans are creatures of habit because following familiar patterns allows the brain to operate efficiently. When you follow these patterns—the way you typically run meetings, handle conflicts, or make decisions—your brain can cruise along on autopilot. It even rewards you with little hits of satisfaction for sticking to familiar patterns, even when those patterns aren't serving you well.

This explains why organizations get stuck in soul-crushing meetings, communication breakdowns, and processes that make everyone want to bang their head against the wall.

The EOS tools and disciplines you've learned make perfect sense on paper, but implementing them can feel like trying to pat your head and rub your stomach at the same time. They require people to abandon comfortable (but ineffective) habits in favor of new behaviors that initially feel about as natural as writing with your non-dominant hand.

THE JOURNEY TO NEW HABITS

Most people aren't wired to tolerate discomfort for extended periods, which is why they often revert to old habits when new behaviors feel challenging. Permanent behavior change requires practicing new behaviors repeatedly until they become comfortable habits—a process that can take anywhere from days to weeks. This is where leadership persistence becomes crucial—maintaining consistency even when people want to give up on new approaches.

Think back to your first Level 10 Meeting. Did you struggle to "drop down" issues instead of diving into lengthy discussions during Scorecard review? Did saying simply "On Track" or "Off Track" feel like you were being rudely brief? Did prioritizing issues feel weird when your brain wanted to just start at the top of the list like always?

Now compare that experience to your current Level 10 Meetings. If you've been running EOS for months or years, these meetings probably feel as natural as breathing—so natural that the thought of going back to your old three-hour discussion marathons makes you shudder.

This transformation illustrates how persistence and repetition can rewire even the most stubborn behavioral patterns.

Your team will experience the same evolution, but they'll need the same time and practice that you required.

THE FOUR STAGES OF LEARNING

Martin Broadwell's "Four Stages of Learning" model helps explain what you experienced as you began implementing EOS, and what your team may experience during Rollout. People follow a natural progression as they learn new skills and assimilate information:

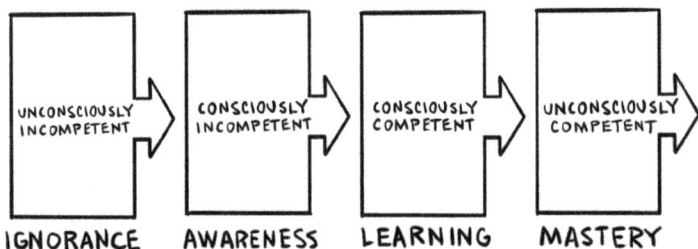

| UNCONSCIOUSLY INCOMPETENT | CONSCIOUSLY INCOMPETENT | CONSCIOUSLY COMPETENT | UNCONSCIOUSLY COMPETENT |
| IGNORANCE | AWARENESS | LEARNING | MASTERY |

Stage 1: Unconsciously Incompetent (Ignorance)
   People don't even know what they don't know; they haven't yet recognized that their current approaches could be improved. They may be skeptical about the need for change.

Stage 2: Consciously Incompetent (Awareness)
   People know what they don't know; they understand that EOS could help, but they feel uncertain about their ability to master new skills. This stage often creates anxiety or resistance.

Stage 3: Consciously Competent (Learning)
   People know what they know; they feel confident and can use EOS tools effectively, but they must think deliberately

about how to apply them. This stage requires encouragement and patience.

Stage 4: Unconsciously Competent (Mastery)
What people know is so ingrained in their habits that they don't even think about it. They use EOS tools naturally and can help others learn. They become internal champions for the system.

As you prepare for Rollout, remember that while you may be comfortably cruising in Stage 3 or 4 of EOS mastery, your team is still back at Stage 1, wondering what the heck you're talking about.

They'll need patient guidance through each stage, and the process will take time. Your brain may have conveniently forgotten the initial excitement, confusion, and occasional "What have we gotten ourselves into?" moments of learning EOS, but your team is about to experience the full emotional rollercoaster.

PREPARING FOR HUMAN NATURE

Recognizing that physiological and behavioral challenges are normal—not deficiencies in your people or your Rollout Plan—enables you to prepare strategically rather than react emotionally.

Resistance to change exists on a spectrum. While many team members will approach EOS with enthusiasm, others may seem overwhelmed or disengaged. Both responses are normal and predictable.

COMMON SOURCES OF RESISTANCE

- **Previous Change Fatigue:** "We've tried so many new initiatives over the years. How do we know this one will stick?"

- **Fear of Increased Accountability:** "Will these new tools be used to micromanage me or catch me making mistakes?"

- **Comfort with Status Quo:** "Our current approach isn't perfect, but at least I know how to succeed within it."

- **Overwhelm:** "I'm already busy with my regular responsibilities. When will I find time to learn all these new things?"

- **Skepticism About Leadership:** "Do our leaders really believe in this, or is it just the latest management fad?"

- **Identity Protection:** "I've built my career on certain skills and approaches. Will I still be valuable in this new system?"

You may have experienced similar emotions when starting your own EOS journey, and you might even be feeling some of them now as you lead this Rollout. This resistance isn't personal—it's simply humans being human.

Thousands of companies running on EOS have navigated these same challenges and emerged stronger. Understanding this reality allows you to approach resistance with empathy and strategic patience rather than frustration or the urge to force compliance.

RESISTANCE AS INFORMATION

Instead of viewing resistance as an obstacle to overcome, try viewing it as valuable information about your Rollout approach. When people seem resistant, they're often telling you:

- **The pace is too fast:** "I need more time to understand before moving to implementation."
- **The context is unclear:** "I don't understand why this change is necessary or how it benefits me."
- **The support is insufficient:** "I want to succeed but don't know how to develop these new skills."
- **The stakes feel too high:** "I'm afraid of failing publicly or losing credibility with my colleagues."

Addressing the underlying concerns that drive resistance is often more effective than trying to push through it.

IF NOTHING CHANGES, NOTHING CHANGES

You started implementing EOS because you wanted something different for your organization—more profit, fewer people problems, better control, improved work-life balance, sustainable growth, or simply a more fulfilling work experience.

These goals are absolutely worth the effort required to achieve them. Sure, change can be hard and a little scary, but there's a fundamental truth that's both obvious and profound: **If nothing changes, nothing changes.**

You can't control how every individual will react to the transformation you've started. Some people will surprise you with their enthusiasm and rapid adoption. Others will be exactly as resistant as you expect. A few may ultimately decide that your new culture isn't the right fit for them.

You can, however, control how you prepare for and respond to these predictable human reactions. The psychological realities we've explored aren't roadblocks to overcome—they're simply the terrain you'll navigate, like knowing there are hills on your running route.

REAL-WORLD PERSPECTIVE: THE JOURNEY IS WORTH IT

Diana Dailey, Integrator at Global Parts & Maintenance, captures this reality perfectly:

> Having a leadership team with buy-in means something. When you start hearing from departmental teams that they see the benefits of EOS, that's when you know it's working. Rejection was a fear—and it happened. But there are no failures—just valuable experiences—and with each challenge, we get better. No one said the journey was going to be easy, but seeing positive changes in the company proves that every bit of effort is worth it. In the past, a lack of organization and accountability meant that a small group of individuals consistently carried the weight. Now that we have EOS, there's structure and clarity, and accountability is shared. Chaos has been replaced with focus and direction.

MOVING FORWARD WITH INTENTION

Understanding why Rollout is hard positions you to approach it strategically rather than hoping it will be easier than it actually is.

In the chapters ahead, we'll explore how to:

- **Build repetition and spaced learning** into your Rollout Plan.
- **Work with human psychology** rather than against it.
- **Create early wins** that build momentum and confidence.
- **Address resistance** with empathy and clear communication.
- **Maintain patience** while holding people accountable for progress.

The same principles that made EOS work for the leadership team will make it work for your entire organization. Your team is ready for this transformation, even if they don't know it yet. And with proper preparation and realistic expectations, you're ready to guide them through it successfully.

Remember: The goal isn't to eliminate the challenges of change; it's to navigate them skillfully so you can achieve the extraordinary results that make the journey worthwhile.

CHAPTER 3 SUMMARY

Changing beliefs and behaviors requires rewiring billions of neural connections, which feels uncomfortable and requires significant mental energy. Your team will need the same patience, repetition, and time you required to develop EOS fluency, and resistance often provides valuable information about pace, context, support needs, or perceived stakes. Understanding why Rollout is inherently difficult will help you approach it with the right expectations, strategies, and mindset by recognizing three core realities:

- **Changing long-held beliefs requires time and repetition** as people learn to look at your business and way of operating through a different lens.

- **Creating new habits demands sustained practice** as people progress through predictable stages from unconscious incompetence to unconscious competence.

- **Understanding resistance as normal helps you respond strategically** rather than emotionally. Common sources include previous change fatigue, fear of increased accountability, comfort with the status quo, overwhelm, skepticism about leadership's commitment, and concerns about identity protection.

The fundamental truth remains: If nothing changes, nothing changes. You can't control individual reactions, but you can control how you prepare for and respond to predictable human responses. The psychological realities of change aren't roadblocks to overcome; they're simply the terrain you'll navigate skillfully to achieve extraordinary results that make the journey worthwhile.

Understanding why Rollout is challenging prepares you to approach it with realistic expectations and strategic patience. The next step is moving beyond obstacle awareness to honestly assess whether your organization is ready to navigate these challenges successfully. Just as a pilot runs through pre-flight checks before takeoff, you need to evaluate your readiness before launching your Rollout. This isn't about achieving perfection; it's about identifying and strengthening any weak spots that could derail your progress once you begin.

What's Next: As leaders responsible for driving EOS Rollout, you've learned what it involves and why it's challenging (Setting the Stage). Next begins the Preparation phase—ensuring you're truly ready to lead this transformation before you start.

In Chapter 4, we'll help you assess your organization's readiness for Rollout by evaluating your EOS foundation, communication readiness, and leadership alignment.

REFLECTION QUESTIONS

1. **Resistance Preparation**: Given our team's personalities and past experiences, what specific types of resistance should we expect during Rollout? Which team members might struggle most with the changes, and why?

2. **Our Own Change Journey**: Reflecting on our own EOS learning experience, what moments did we feel most resistant or overwhelmed? How can understanding our own journey help us be more patient with our team's process?

3. **Mindset Check**: Are we approaching this Rollout from a place of excitement about the possibilities, or anxiety about the challenges? How might our mindset influence how our team receives and responds to the changes?

4

GETTING READY FOR ROLLOUT

A workman who wants to do his
work well must first sharpen his tools.

—Confucius

After months of intensive work—clarifying the vision, building your Accountability Chart, mastering new tools and disciplines, and wrestling with people issues—the leadership team has reached a crucial milestone. You've done the hard work of getting clear on where you're going and how you'll get there. The EOS tools are becoming second nature in your leadership team meetings.

Now comes the exciting part: sharing the vision and EOS with the rest of the organization. (And yes, we said "exciting"—though it might not feel that way at first.)

Before you step in front of your team to cast the vision and introduce EOS, it's time for an honest assessment of your readiness for rollout. Think of this as your pre-flight check— not because we expect everything to be perfect, but because we want to identify any critical gaps that could derail your Rollout before it begins.

As EOS Implementers, we start planting these seeds during Vision Building Day 2, helping leadership teams think through the need for a Rollout Plan rather than just winging it. Remember, there is no universally "right" way to roll out EOS. Every company is different and chooses a different path based on its unique circumstances, culture, and challenges.

What matters most is that the leadership team is genuinely aligned on the approach and committed to executing the plan they've developed together.

THE MOMENT OF TRUTH

As you start thinking about introducing the vision and EOS to the rest of the company, you're likely experiencing what might be called "Rollout butterflies"—that familiar mix of emotions every leadership team faces at this stage.

- **Excitement** about the transformation ahead and the potential impact on your organization.
- **Anxiety** about how your team will respond to change and new expectations.
- **Pride** in the work you've accomplished and the vision you've created.
- **Worry** about your ability to execute this Rollout effectively.
- **Impatience** to start seeing results throughout the entire organization.
- **Fear** about resistance, confusion, or implementation challenges ahead.

This emotional cocktail is completely normal and actually a good sign. It means you understand the significance of what you're about to do.

You know you won't really start to gain traction if you don't get everyone else on board with the vision and EOS. The leadership team's alignment is necessary but not sufficient for organizational transformation. You need the entire choir singing in harmony, not just the section leaders.

Yet you're also worried. A million questions are racing around in your head:

- Will the next-level leaders be able to get their teams to adopt Level 10 Meetings?
- Will Aliya in accounting accept her new role as Controller?
- Are our people going to feel like we're micro-managing them with Measurables?
- What about all those tough conversations we need to have with the Right People Right Seats issues we've identified?
- How will we handle the skeptics who think this is just another "flavor-of-the-month" initiative?

You've been working on this vision for three months—a long time to keep major decisions private. Perhaps you're feeling like you've been a little secretive, holding back information that could help your team perform better.

This internal tension between readiness and worry is exactly where you should be right now. It demonstrates that you take this responsibility seriously and understand the impact your leadership will have on everyone in the organization.

Let's focus on the promise ahead. The vision you've created isn't just words on paper; it's a roadmap for your organization's future. The clarity you've gained around structure, roles, and priorities will eliminate confusion and create focus. The EOS tools and disciplines you're preparing to implement will drive results like never before.

One essential step remains: making sure you're truly ready.

THE FIVE KEY ROLLOUT READINESS QUESTIONS

Here are the questions that will help you decide if you're ready to begin Rollout or need to shore up your foundation first:

1. Has the leadership team mastered the five EOS Foundational Tools (V/TO, The Accountability Chart, Rocks, The Meeting Pulse, Scorecard)?
2. Are you ready to share your EOS tools with the organization?
3. Are you ready to present a united front as a leadership team?
4. Are you ready to be open and honest with your team?
5. Are you ready to shift from student to teacher?

Before we examine each readiness area, let's clarify some key terms we'll use throughout this book. We'll refer to "departments" as groups of people who work together regularly and share responsibilities—typically organized around major functions like Sales, Operations, or Finance, but sometimes around locations, divisions, business units, etc. We'll also discuss "mid-managers"—the people outside the leadership team who manage their own teams.

Let's examine each question in detail.

1. HAS THE LEADERSHIP TEAM "MASTERED" THE EOS FOUNDATIONAL TOOLS?

First, let's be clear about what "mastered" means here. We're not talking about perfection; we're talking about competence and consistency. You don't need to be an EOS black belt, but you do need to be actively using these tools and seeing positive results.

Rolling out EOS successfully requires that the leadership team understands the five EOS Foundational Tools (V/TO, The Accountability Chart, Rocks, The Meeting Pulse, and Scorecard) and uses them daily.

Here's what "ready" looks like at the leadership team level.

VISION/TRACTION ORGANIZER® (V/TO®)

Before rolling out EOS to your organization, the leadership team must be aligned on the answers to the 8 Questions on the V/TO and genuinely excited about your vision. If the leadership team isn't authentically enthusiastic, your organization will sense that immediately, and your Rollout will struggle from the beginning.

Even though the entire leadership team participated in answering the 8 Questions on the V/TO, you may still be struggling with consistency. Some leaders might remember Core Values better than others, while someone else may always explain the 10-Year Target differently, and not everyone feels equally passionate about every aspect yet. Some days you'll make decisions that perfectly align with your V/TO, while other days you'll realize afterward that you defaulted to old habits.

This is completely normal. Your alignment will strengthen over time as you progress through the EOS Process and engage in the 90-Day World®. Remember that your V/TO becomes the foundation for everything else in EOS. Get this foundation right, and everything else becomes significantly easier. Rush this step, and you'll spend months trying to recover from a shaky foundation.

To gauge whether you're ready, ask yourself:

- **Does your vision make your heart beat faster?** When you think about achieving your 10-Year Target, 3-Year Picture, and 1-Year Plan, do you feel energized?

- **Does it give you a sense of purpose?** Can you connect your daily work to something meaningful and worthwhile?

- **Do you feel the weight of possibility?** When you imagine your organization at 80+ percent strong, does it seem like a place where you'd want to work and build your career?

If your answer is yes, then you're ready for the next step.

If your answer is no or you're feeling uncertain, pause here. A lukewarm leadership team will create a lukewarm Rollout.

Consider spending more time refining the vision or working through leadership team alignment issues before proceeding.

Remember, even if your V/TO isn't perfect, it's probably ready if the leadership team is truly committed to it and can communicate it consistently. The vision will continue to evolve and strengthen as you live it and breathe it together. The key isn't perfection; it's progress and commitment.

READINESS ASSESSMENT QUESTIONS: V/TO

- Have you completed all 8 sections of the V/TO?
- Is every leader genuinely excited about this vision?
- Does every leader understand and believe in every word of the V/TO?
- Can you imagine the impact the V/TO will have when everyone knows where the company is going and how you're going to get there?

THE ACCOUNTABILITY CHART®

Creating your Accountability Chart was likely one of your most challenging exercises, requiring difficult conversations about organizational structure and people decisions—the kind that make even seasoned leaders want to hide under their desks.

The transformation during your first three EOS sessions was significant. You established a leadership structure with clearly defined positions—Visionary, Integrator, and key functional roles—and placed people in these seats. You may have experienced a complete redefinition of your roles and responsibilities, which is a substantial shift to absorb in a relatively short timeframe.

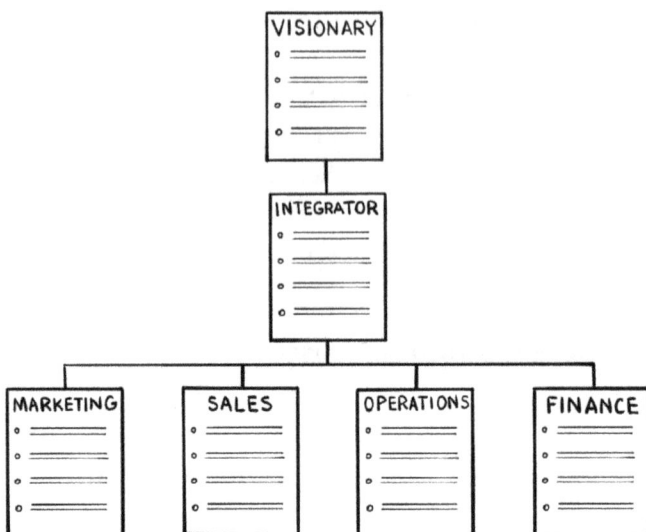

Your Accountability Chart is a living document that will require continued updates as people come and go, and will continue to evolve as your business grows. Before sharing The Accountability Chart with your team, the leadership team must:

- **Commit to the structure.** Step back from individual people and focus on the structure. Is this the clearest and simplest structure to help us grow and scale the business? Does it create role clarity and help people understand who is accountable for what? If a new person were dropped into your organization, would they know who to go to for their specific needs?

- **Commit to getting the Right People into the Right Seats.** Remember, Right People means filling your organization with people who share your core values. Right Seats means ensuring that every person Gets it, Wants it, and has the Capacity to do the job. You may have identified some Right Person/Wrong Seat or Wrong Person/Right Seat issues while building your Accountability Chart, and you must commit to resolving these issues as they arise.

- **Commit to solving your capacity issues.** Many teams also discover they've been wearing multiple hats without adequate time capacity to reach the next level—an issue that should resolve naturally as you learn to delegate and address your people challenges in a timely manner.

As Gino Wickman often states, "The root of all evil is in The Accountability Chart." When you solve your structural and people issues effectively throughout the organization, you will break through ceilings more quickly. This is why your commitment to actively and consistently using The Accountability Chart as a tool over the coming quarters will determine your success with the entire EOS system.

READINESS ASSESSMENT QUESTIONS: ACCOUNTABILITY CHART

- Are you committed to this organizational structure, even if you're not certain yet?
- Do you have a plan to address any remaining Right People Right Seats issues?
- Does everyone on the leadership team understand their role in the new structure?
- Are you committed to devoting the time necessary to lead and manage your people?
- Can you imagine the impact The Accountability Chart will have on the rest of the team when everyone is clear on who is accountable for what?

ROCKS

Let's address the elephant in the room: Your first round of Rocks was essentially a practice set. If you're like most teams, you probably achieved only 30–60 percent completion of your company and individual Rocks in your first quarter.

```
┌─────────────────────────────────────┐
│              ROCKS                   │
├─────────────────────────────────────┤
│  FUTURE DATE·                        │
│  REVENUE:                            │
│  PROFIT:                             │
│  MEASURABLES :                       │
│                                      │
│  ROCKS FOR THE QUARTER      WHO      │
│  ┌──┬──────────────────────┬──────┐  │
│  │1.│                      │      │  │
│  ├──┼──────────────────────┼──────┤  │
│  │2.│                      │      │  │
│  ├──┼──────────────────────┼──────┤  │
│  │3.│                      │      │  │
│  ├──┼──────────────────────┼──────┤  │
│  │4.│                      │      │  │
│  ├──┼──────────────────────┼──────┤  │
│  │5.│                      │      │  │
│  ├──┼──────────────────────┼──────┤  │
│  │6.│                      │      │  │
│  ├──┼──────────────────────┼──────┤  │
│  │7.│                      │      │  │
│  └──┴──────────────────────┴──────┘  │
└─────────────────────────────────────┘
```

Before you start beating yourself up, take a deep breath. That's completely normal and expected. It often takes two to three quarters for leadership teams to feel truly confident in their Rock setting.

The real value in your first quarter wasn't necessarily in what you accomplished, but in what you learned. Sometimes it's a "winning" quarter, sometimes it's a "learning" quarter. It's essential that you conduct a complete debrief at the end of each quarter to identify what went well and what didn't when setting and achieving your Rocks. This is how you achieve mastery.

COMMON FIRST-QUARTER ROCK CHALLENGES

In the first quarter, most leadership teams experience these growing pains:

- **Overcommitting**—Taking on too many Rocks or misjudging the scope, time, and resources required
- **Writing vague Rocks**—Missing the S.M.A.R.T. (Specific, Measurable, Attainable, Realistic, Timely) criteria that make it clear what a Rock really looks like when it's "Done"
- **Poor planning and communication**—Failing to monitor progress or alert the team when Rocks go off-track until it's too late
- **Last-minute scrambling**—Rushing to complete Rocks at quarter-end, often claiming they're "done" when they're not quite finished

If this sounds familiar, welcome to the club. Every successful EOS team has been exactly where you are right now.

THE LEARNING CURVE

Think back on what you learned during that first quarter. Would you have gained the same insights into priority-setting, resource allocation, and follow-through if you hadn't experienced the sometimes-painful failure to complete your Rocks?

In just one quarter, you moved from unconsciously incompetent (not knowing what you didn't know about executing

Rocks) to consciously incompetent (now aware of what you need to improve). That's genuine progress that will serve you well in future quarters.

Over the coming quarters, you'll notice something powerful happening. You'll begin emerging from your departmental silos and start helping each other get Rocks across the finish line. You'll stop thinking "That's not my Rock" and start thinking "That's our Rock that's not getting done." This shift represents the true formation of your leadership team's identity.

Your organization will be watching how seriously you take your own Rocks. If the leadership team doesn't demonstrate Rock discipline, why should anyone else?

READINESS ASSESSMENT QUESTIONS: ROCKS

- Are you consistently setting Rocks that are truly S.M.A.R.T. (Specific, Measurable, Attainable, Realistic, Timely)?
- Are team members comfortable speaking up when Rocks go off-track?
- Are you using IDS to solve Rock-related issues and get things back on track?
- Are you learning from both completed and incomplete Rocks?
- Can you imagine the impact that Rocks will have when everyone is getting 80 percent or more done every quarter?

THE MEETING PULSE®

Looking at The Meeting Pulse is like reading an EKG—it shows the vital signs of your organization's health. When your meetings are strong, information flows freely, issues get resolved quickly, and everyone stays aligned. When they're weak, communication breaks down, problems fester, and progress stalls.

Creating this healthy cadence starts with the leadership team and then extends throughout the organization. Now that you've been meeting regularly as a leadership team, establishing a meeting pulse in your next-level departments is critical to gaining traction company-wide. Before you begin implementing meetings across the company, make sure your own meeting pulse is functioning well.

L-10 MEETINGS

LEVEL 10 MEETING®

The Level 10 Meeting has the potential to be the biggest impact tool in the entire EOS Toolbox. That said, let's be honest about where most teams are at this stage: your Level 10 Meetings are probably still developing, and that's completely normal.

In our experience, only a handful of teams have truly effective leadership team Level 10 Meetings at the time of Rollout. Most teams are still figuring it out, learning to stay on agenda, discovering what issues are worth bringing up, and getting comfortable with the IDS process. Some weeks feel productive, while others feel like you're going through the motions.

Here's what we typically see in those first few quarters:

- People are still bringing up issues that aren't really issues (more like updates or complaints)
- Getting stuck in discussion mode instead of actually solving things
- Scorecard reviews that turn into lengthy explanations
- To-dos that never get done
- Getting lost in rabbit holes or tangents during IDS
- Awkward silences when you ask, "Do you have any issues to add?"
- Spending time on departmental-level issues or people issues that aren't being solved by individual members of the leadership team

Sound familiar? You're in good company. The key question isn't whether your Level 10 Meetings are amazing yet; it's whether you're committed to making them better each week. Most teams need two to three quarters to really hit their stride with Level 10 Meetings. The magic happens gradually as people start bringing up better issues, conversations become more focused, and you begin to see real problems getting solved instead of just discussed.

QUARTERLY AND ANNUAL PLANNING

While Level 10 Meetings keep you connected and accountable week by week, the 90-Day World of Quarterlies and Annuals is where the real magic happens—this is where you gain and maintain true traction.

As you progress through the EOS Process, you'll meet quarterly and annually as a leadership team to realign, refocus, and recommit to the vision. Eventually, you'll also do quarterly and annual planning at the department level (more on this in Chapter 7). These planning sessions are where you step back from the day-to-day operations to work *on* your business rather than just *in* it.

Committing to quarterly and annual planning meetings is a big adjustment for most entrepreneurial leaders. These aren't typical business meetings; they demand your complete presence and focus. Remaining fully engaged while the team works through the agenda can feel challenging when the outside world beckons. Phone calls, texts, "emergency" sales meetings, and countless other distractions will try to pull you away from what is actually the most important day of your quarter.

As a team, you must hold each other accountable to honor the time commitment you've all made. This discipline at the leadership level sets the tone for the entire organization. If leaders can't protect their most important meetings, how can they expect their teams to do the same?

When the leadership team consistently maintains this Meeting Pulse—weekly Level 10 Meetings, quarterly planning, and annual sessions—the impact becomes transformative. Your teams will see the power of focused, productive meetings and eagerly adopt the same disciplines. Remember: Vision without Traction is hallucination.

READINESS ASSESSMENT QUESTIONS: MEETING PULSE

- Are you holding Level 10 Meetings every week, on the same day, at the same time, without exception?
- Does everyone show up on time, stay engaged, and contribute meaningfully?
- Are you sticking to the agenda and resisting the urge to go down rabbit holes?

- Are you actually solving issues using IDS, not just talking about them?
- Are To-dos from meetings getting completed before the next meeting?

SCORECARD

Is your Scorecard built, and are you consistently tracking your weekly Measurables? If it's not perfect yet—and it probably isn't—that's completely normal. It's very common for it to take one to three months for teams to fall in love with their Scorecard, and it will continue to evolve as the business grows. Here's why that timeline is actually healthy.

WHO	MEASURABLES	GOAL	1/5	1/12	1/19	1/26	2/2	2/9	2/16	2/23	3/1	3/8	3/15	3/22	3/29

YOU'RE LEARNING WHICH NUMBERS MATTER

When you established your Scorecard Measurables during Focus Day, you were making educated guesses about what numbers would be important to track weekly. Even though these guesses were based on significant experience, they were still guesses.

As you've gone through your weekly Level 10 Meetings, you've likely discovered that some of these Measurables are "nice to know" numbers rather than "need to know" numbers. They don't spark meaningful conversation, drive important decisions, or help you identify problems before they become bigger issues.

The real discipline comes in being willing to stop tracking the "nice to know" data points. Every week, when a Measurable doesn't spark conversation or drive action, your team should drop it into your Issues List. Ask the hard question: "Is this number actually helping us make better decisions, or are we just tracking it because we can?"

The Measurables that truly matter—the "canary in the coal mine" numbers that predict problems before they happen—will reveal themselves over time.

YOU'RE BUILDING THE INFRASTRUCTURE

Beyond identifying the right numbers, you're also building the infrastructure to capture them. The other reason your Scorecard might take time to perfect is more practical: getting reliable numbers can be more challenging than you initially anticipated. Identifying what you want to track is the easy part. Developing the systems and processes to capture that data weekly—and capture it accurately—takes time, iteration, and problem-solving.

Don't let this discourage you. Your team needs to see you living by data rather than just gut feelings and good intentions. They also need to see that you're figuring it out as you go, making adjustments, and continuously improving the process. That's not a weakness—that's leadership in action. There's a big difference between raw data and useful INFORMATION that improves our knowledge about what's behind the numbers, which is why a great Scorecard takes time.

This infrastructure work matters because your Scorecard isn't decoration. It's your early warning system, your progress tracker, and your accountability partner all rolled into one. If it's not serving those purposes yet, keep refining it until it does.

The discipline you demonstrate with your leadership team's Scorecard will set the standard for every Scorecard that follows in your organization. When you show genuine commitment to using data to drive decisions and actions, your teams will follow that example throughout the company.

*⚲ **Mastery Tip:** For more depth on Scorecards, consider reading the book* Data *by Mark O'Donnell, Mark Stanley, and Angela Kalemis, published in 2025 as part of the EOS Mastery series.*

READINESS ASSESSMENT QUESTIONS: SCORECARD

- Are you reviewing your Scorecard every week without fail?
- Do the numbers actually drive meaningful conversations and decisions?
- Can you trust the data you're seeing each week?
- When numbers are off track, do you dig into why and take corrective action?
- Are you willing to adjust Measurables that aren't adding value?
- Does each leadership team member own their numbers and take responsibility for results?

---

2. ARE YOU READY TO SHARE THE EOS FOUNDATIONAL TOOLS?

Don't let perfectionist thinking dissuade you from moving forward. You don't have to be perfectly aligned as a leadership team, and your five EOS Foundational Tools don't have to be perfect to start rolling out your vision and EOS to the team.

That said, the leadership team does need to understand the tools and use them consistently to provide clear direction for your organization. Think of it like teaching your kids to ride a bike—you don't need to be a professional cyclist, but you do need to know how to ride and be able to explain the basics.

Remember that your organization will model what they see, not what they hear. Make sure what they see is worth copying. As your organization evolves over time, your vision and EOS tools will evolve too. Every quarter, you'll review your V/TO, your Accountability Chart, your Rocks, and Scorecard to make the adjustments needed to gain traction toward your vision.

That said, if a tool feels particularly shaky or uncertain, it's perfectly fine to wait a quarter or two before rolling it out to the rest of your company. Better to avoid unnecessary confusion than to rush ahead and create problems. Sometimes, readiness means slowing down just a bit to go faster later.

READINESS ASSESSMENT QUESTIONS: SHARING YOUR TOOLS

- Are we ready to share the entire V/TO, or should we introduce it section by section over time?

- Is The Accountability Chart ready to be distributed, or are there still some sensitive conversations that need to happen first?

- Are Rocks something we want to roll out immediately, or would it be better to wait a quarter or two until we've demonstrated more consistency and proficiency?

- Would certain teams benefit from having Level 10 Meetings immediately, while other teams might need more preparation?

> - Are Scorecards really important right out of the gate, or do we need to make sure our data reporting is accurate at the leadership team level first?

3. ARE YOU READY TO PRESENT A UNITED FRONT?

Once you introduce these tools, the rest of your organization will look to you for consistency. If your leaders aren't saying the same thing, using the same language, and modeling the same behavior, the Rollout will feel confusing—or worse, performative. Nothing undermines leadership effectiveness faster than mixed messages from the top.

You must present a united front, even if you're not feeling like you're 100 percent on the same page yet. This requires both courage and intentionality. Sometimes that means having difficult leadership team conversations to achieve alignment before facing your organization.

THE CHALLENGE OF BECOMING A LEADERSHIP TEAM

For many of our clients, thinking of themselves as a leadership team is a new, sometimes uncomfortable concept, even after three months of discussing it. This language shift was introduced during Focus Day, when you learned about the journey to becoming your best. By committing to becoming a leadership team, you've established ground rules for how the leadership team is meant to behave together.

Later in the day, when the Visionary, Integrator, and functional leaders are identified, that leadership team actually comes to life, and the rewiring of everyone's brains in that room begins. Over the next two sessions, team members are getting used to the new structure and the responsibilities that come with it. It's a lot to process.

THE POWER OF LANGUAGE IN LEADERSHIP

Leadership is fundamentally about taking responsibility for how your actions and words affect the lives of others. Language doesn't just describe your organization's reality—it actively shapes it.

In addition to all this structural rewiring, you're being asked to behave as a unified group, with no visible cracks. For many teams where politics and organizational silos have been ongoing issues, shifting to a healthy paradigm begins with consciously choosing new language patterns.

The language shifts are both strategic and symbolic.

- Using EOS terms consistently ("The Accountability Chart" instead of "Org Chart," etc.)
- Using "we" more frequently instead of defaulting to "I" language when discussing team decisions
- Being intentional about how you talk about each other to the rest of the organization
- Speaking consistently about priorities, challenges, and opportunities
- Talking about "our vision" rather than "my vision" or "the company's vision"

You may not think much of these subtle changes, but at a subconscious level, these words start to shape minds and perceptions. Your organization is listening not just to what you say, but how you say it and what that reveals about your actual unity.

📋 *Rollout Planning Tip: Try having each leader practice explaining EOS concepts to the leadership team. If explanations vary significantly, it's worth spending more time aligning before you launch. You could also try creating a "cheat sheet" with talking points to help leaders use consistent language.*

ONE VISION. ONE VOICE. ONE TEAM.

Achieving perfect alignment isn't always immediate, and that's completely normal. It may take several quarters for the leadership team to feel like a unified team, rowing in the same direction with natural synchronization.

It's not uncommon for this to feel like "false harmony" at the beginning—and that discomfort actually signals growth, not failure. You're learning new ways of working together, and that always feels awkward before it feels natural.

While we always encourage leaders to be open and honest, this might be one area where the organization needs to see consistency before it's felt internally. Your commitment to unified language and messaging, even during the awkward early stages, creates the foundation for authentic alignment to emerge over time.

By using the EOS tools consistently and being intentional about your language choices, you will eventually fall into lock-step naturally. Trust the process—it works, but it takes time and deliberate practice.

☞ *Mastery Tip: If the Visionary and Integrator seats in your company are held by two separate people, consider reading* Rocket Fuel *by Gino Wickman and Mark C. Winters to strengthen this critical partnership. The Same Page Meeting discipline outlined in that book helps ensure these two key roles stay aligned throughout the Rollout process.*

READINESS ASSESSMENT QUESTIONS: UNITED FRONT

- Is every leader using consistent language?
- Are we committed to supporting each other publicly, even when we disagree privately?
- Have we worked through any significant conflicts or trust issues between team members?
- Do we agree on how to handle questions we can't answer immediately?

---

4. ARE YOU READY TO BE OPEN AND HONEST?

The leadership team's mindset about Rollout is absolutely critical to success. If you approach Rollout with scarcity and fear instead of abundance and love, you're going to have a much harder time and get less satisfying results.

Rolling out your vision and EOS demands transparency and an abundance mindset—a willingness to trust your team with the truth about where the company stands, where it's headed, and what challenges lie ahead.

Embracing this transparency doesn't come naturally to most leaders, particularly owners and founders. We get it—vulnerability in leadership can feel risky, especially when you're not sure how people will react. And here's what we've learned: Your people are desperately waiting for you to trust them with the truth.

SCARCITY AND FEAR

Humans are wired for scarcity thinking. It's how we've survived for thousands of years. As a species, we're really good at spotting threats, and our brains and nervous systems are designed to protect our families and us from anything dangerous.

The problem is that the survival instinct doesn't help us in business. When we treat everything as a threat—including the people on our team—we end up creating the very problems we're worried about. We've gotten smarter as a species, but we haven't gotten better at managing our emotions. And that disconnect shows up constantly in how we lead.

When fear and scarcity drive your Rollout, you'll find yourself:

- Holding back critical information that could help people make better decisions

- Sugar-coating difficult truths about performance, competition, or market conditions

- Trying to control every aspect of the Rollout process instead of trusting your team

- Worrying excessively about what people will think or how they'll react

- Second-guessing whether your team can handle the full picture of where the company stands

Here's the thing: your people WANT transparency. They're desperate for it. In the absence of transparency, people will often create their own narratives, which are often not a reflection of the leadership team's true desires and motivations.

You've hired capable, intelligent, and talented adults who need their leaders to make the bold move to do something differently—to act with the greater good of the business and the people within it in mind.

Don't let fear stop you from becoming the best version of yourselves as leaders.

ABUNDANCE AND LOVE

Ask most truly successful people how they became successful, and they'll say things like, "I learned to let go," "I trusted my team," "I focused on helping people grow and succeed." Success isn't pie—there's not a limited amount to go around. Success comes from adopting an abundance mindset and embracing the idea that the more you 'put the love in it,' the more you will get in return.

This isn't about giving to get or manipulating people through false generosity. Success is a delightful by-product of an abundance mindset, not the primary goal itself.

During Focus Day, we compared great leaders to great parents. According to Thomas Gordon, author of *Parent Effectiveness Training*, great parents have a handful of clear rules, repeat themselves often, and remain consistent in their expectations and behavior.[2] Great leaders do the same thing: Your core values are your handful of rules. You'll often repeat yourself as you teach the EOS Process and tools to your teams. You'll need to be consistent with Rocks, Level 10 Meetings, and all the other disciplines, even when things get hard.

Think about the best attributes of your parents, favorite teachers, or most respected mentors. Didn't they approach their teaching and guidance with genuine care and abundance? They believed in your potential, even when you couldn't see it yourself. They shared knowledge freely, trusted you to learn from mistakes, and celebrated your growth along the way.

This is the mindset that makes Rollout powerful and transformative. When you approach your team with genuine care for their success, transparency about challenges, and confidence in their ability to rise to the occasion, you create an environment where EOS can truly thrive.

An abundance mindset in Rollout means:

- Sharing the full vision, including the challenges and obstacles ahead
- Trusting your team with complete transparency about company performance and market conditions
- Believing that everyone can learn and grow with the right tools and support
- Focusing on collective success rather than protecting individual territories or egos
- Embracing the messiness of learning and improvement rather than demanding perfection

When you consistently embrace this abundance mindset, you naturally shift from being a student of EOS to a teacher— and that transformation is exactly what your organization needs from you now.

Mastery Tip: For more depth on leading with an abundance mindset, consider reading People *by Mark O'Donnell, Kelly Knight, and CJ Dubé, published in 2024 as part of the EOS Mastery series.*

READINESS ASSESSMENT QUESTIONS: OPEN & HONEST

- Are we genuinely committed to transparency, even when it feels uncomfortable?

- Do we trust our team with the truth about our challenges and opportunities?

- Are we prepared to admit when we don't know something or when we make mistakes?

- Can we focus on collective success rather than individual credit or blame?

- Are we willing to be vulnerable in service of the organization's growth?

---

5. ARE YOU READY TO SHIFT FROM STUDENT TO TEACHER?

Here's where things get both exciting and a little daunting. You've spent the last several months learning EOS—and now you're about to teach it to others.

This shift is intentional and necessary. Rollout is fundamentally a train-the-trainer model by design. This work can't be outsourced to someone outside the organization; it's an inside job that your team has to do, or it simply won't work.

This is what being "good parents" to your employees means. You can't hold people accountable for rules they've never heard or expectations they don't understand. You have to teach first—clearly, consistently, and with the same care and patience you'd show your own children.

The truth is, teaching EOS isn't about delivering perfect presentations or having all the answers. Good teaching means explaining why these tools matter, connecting concepts to real problems your team faces, and asking questions to ensure people truly understand rather than just nod along politely. You'll need to check for genuine comprehension, address confusion with patience, and help people connect the dots between EOS concepts and their daily work.

The best EOS teachers are those who create dialogue rather than just talking at people, who admit when they're still learning too, and who focus more on helping people succeed than on looking like experts. (We'll explore specific strategies for effective teaching and checking for understanding in chapters 6 and 7.)

The good news is that teaching deepens your own mastery. Every question your team asks will sharpen your understanding of the concepts. Every stumble will reveal gaps in knowledge you didn't know existed. Every success will reinforce the value of what you're building together.

The better news? You don't have to do it perfectly from the beginning. While you may now be consciously competent in using the EOS tools, you may find yourself feeling consciously incompetent when you think about teaching them. Your job now is simply to begin the teaching process with authenticity and commitment.

SELLING THE BIG PICTURE

Rollout isn't just about teaching EOS; it's about inspiring your people with the big picture of your company's why, where, and how.

You're not just implementing a system or checking boxes on a checklist. You're inviting everyone into a shared future. You're giving them context, clarity, and a meaningful role in something bigger than themselves. When done well, Rollout transforms how every person sees their work—not as tasks to complete or hours to log, but as contributions to a vision they feel connected to and excited about.

This means you need to bring genuine passion to the table—actually, you need to bring all your passion to the table.

READINESS ASSESSMENT QUESTIONS: STUDENT TO TEACHER

- Are we genuinely excited about teaching EOS, not just implementing it?
- Can we explain the "why" behind each tool in compelling terms?
- Are we prepared to answer questions we might not have considered?
- Do we have the patience to explain concepts multiple times in multiple ways?
- Are we committed to modeling what we teach, even when it's difficult?

If you're not there yet, that's okay. This chapter, and this book, are here to help you get there.

THE ROLLOUT CHAMPION AS CONDUCTOR

Just as every great choir needs a skilled conductor to keep everyone in tempo and harmony, a successful Rollout often depends on having a Rollout Champion who can orchestrate the entire process. This role is often filled by the Integrator, who naturally sees the whole organization, understands how all the pieces fit together, and has the execution focus to keep everyone moving in the same direction. That said, the Rollout Champion could be any leader with the right skills and commitment.

Like a conductor, the Rollout Champion doesn't need to be the best singer in the choir, but they must understand the music deeply and have the credibility to guide others. They set the tempo for implementation, cue different departments when it's their turn to engage, and help the entire organization stay synchronized as they learn to work together in harmony.

The conductor-like view is crucial during Rollout because this role requires big-picture, systematic thinking. While other leaders might focus primarily on their own departments, the Rollout Champion sees how departmental Level 10 Meetings need to connect, how Rocks must align across teams, and how Scorecard metrics should work together to create organizational accountability.

If you're serving as the Rollout Champion, remember that Rollout success often rests heavily on your shoulders—not because you have to do everything yourself, but because you're the one ensuring everyone else plays their part skillfully and on time. Trust your instincts about pacing, sequencing, and coordination. Your execution mindset and ability to see how everything connects are exactly what the organization needs to transform from individual contributors into a harmonious, high-performing team.

☞ **Mastery Tip:** *For more information on clarifying the roles of the Visionary and Integrator, read* Rocket Fuel *by Gino Wickman and Mark C. Winters.*

DON'T LET PERFECT BE THE ENEMY OF GOOD

While these readiness questions might seem straightforward, many leadership teams fall into a particular trap: protecting their people from 'too much change.' This protective instinct, while well-intentioned, can become the biggest obstacle to a successful Rollout.

One company's experience illustrates why waiting for the "perfect time" often means never starting at all.

REAL-WORLD EXAMPLE: THE COMPANY THAT WAITED TOO LONG

Professional Benefit Administrators, a 120+ person health care claims processing company, had been running EOS at the leadership level for over a year. Their Level 10 Meetings were solid, their Rocks were getting done, and their Scorecard was finally meaningful. Even so, Jeff Walter, their Visionary, and Christina Alonzo, their Integrator, kept finding reasons to delay Rollout.

"Our team just went through a brutal enterprise software transition," Jeff would explain one quarter. "Let's let them catch their breath first," Christina agreed. "Our mid-managers are already stretched thin—they can't handle another thing right now," became the recurring theme as months turned into years.

The leadership team had developed a protective instinct around their people, born from genuine care and recent organizational trauma. They'd witnessed firsthand how the software implementation had pushed everyone to their limits, and the last thing they wanted was to pile more onto already overwhelmed managers.

Meanwhile, the same frustrations kept surfacing in leadership meetings. Departments were working in silos. Mid-managers were escalating decisions that should have been made at their level. Employees were unclear about priorities and company direction, leading to misaligned efforts and duplicated work.

"Every week, we'd solve issues that should have been handled three levels down," said Christina. "But we kept telling ourselves we needed to wait for the 'right time' when our managers would be ready for more responsibility."

The turning point came during their second annual planning session. Looking back at two full years of EOS at the leadership level, they realized they'd created an unintended consequence: by protecting their team from additional structure and clarity, they'd actually made everyone's job harder.

"We had this lightbulb moment," Jeff reflected. "We were still solving all the departmental issues ourselves because we'd never given our managers the tools to solve them. We thought we were being considerate, but we were actually being overprotective."

The data was undeniable. Despite running EOS successfully at the top, they were still spending 60 percent of their leadership meeting time on issues that belonged at lower levels of the organization. Their managers, while appreciative of the leadership team's support, were frustrated by their inability to make decisions independently.

"We realized we weren't protecting our people—we were limiting them," Christina said. "By waiting for them to be 'ready,' we were denying them the very tools that would make their jobs easier and more fulfilling."

When they finally launched their Rollout—acknowledging that there would never be a perfect time—the results surprised everyone. Rather than adding burden to their mid-managers, EOS gave them clarity, structure, and decision-making authority they'd been craving.

Within 60 days, the issues escalated to the leadership team dropped by 40 percent. Managers who had seemed overwhelmed suddenly had frameworks for prioritizing, problem-solving, and communicating with their teams.

"The irony wasn't lost on us," Jeff said. "We spent two years trying to protect our managers from more responsibility, when what they actually needed were better tools to handle the responsibility they already had."

"There's never going to be a perfect time," Christina added. "We kept waiting for our people to be ready, but we realized we had it backwards—EOS doesn't add burden to people who are already overwhelmed. It gives them the structure and clarity that actually reduces the overwhelm."

CHAPTER 4 SUMMARY

Before rolling out EOS to your organization, conduct an honest readiness assessment across five critical areas. This isn't about perfection; it's about ensuring you have a solid foundation to build upon.

- **Master the EOS Foundational Tools.** The leadership team should be actively using and seeing results from the V/TO, The Accountability Chart, Rocks, The Meeting Pulse, and Scorecard. You don't need to be experts, but you need to demonstrate consistent competence and genuine commitment to each tool.

- **Decide which tools to introduce**. It's perfectly acceptable to phase the introduction of different tools based on your team's readiness and organizational needs.

- **Present a united front.** Your organization will model what they see, not what they hear. Leadership teams must demonstrate consistent language, unified messaging, and aligned behavior, even if perfect internal alignment is still developing.

- **Embrace openness and honesty.** Approach Rollout with an abundance mindset rather than fear and scarcity. Your people want transparency and truth about where the company stands and where it's headed. Trust them with the information they need to succeed.

- **Shift from student to teacher.** There's an old saying: "If you want to learn something, teach it." EOS is a train-the-trainer model by design. You must become internal champions who can teach these tools with authenticity and passion, knowing that teaching will deepen your own mastery.

Remember that readiness doesn't require perfection; it requires commitment, consistency, and the courage to begin. If you can't check every box, focus your energy on strengthening weak areas before proceeding. Your organization will follow your example, so make sure what they see is worth copying.

By considering the readiness assessment questions, you've either confirmed you're prepared to move forward or identified specific areas that need strengthening before you begin. Either way, you now understand what solid preparation looks like. Even the most prepared organizations, however, can stumble without a thoughtful plan that considers their unique circumstances, culture, and capacity for change. Successful Rollout isn't about following a rigid template; it's about creating a strategic approach that fits your specific situation while incorporating proven principles that consistently drive results.

What's Next: In Chapter 5, we'll help you create a comprehensive plan to roll out EOS across your organization, including roles, timelines, and communication.

REFLECTION QUESTIONS

1. **EOS Foundation Assessment**: Which of our five Foundational Tools (V/TO, The Accountability Chart,

Rocks, The Meeting Pulse, Scorecard) feels strongest right now? Which needs the most work before Rollout?

2. **Vision Alignment**: Are we genuinely excited about our vision, or are we just going through the motions? What would it take to move from lukewarm to passionate?

3. **Teaching Readiness**: Are we prepared to teach these tools with authentic enthusiasm? What would help us feel more confident as teachers?

4. **Mindset Check**: Are we approaching this Rollout from a place of abundance and trust, or are we holding back out of fear? What would it look like to be completely transparent with our team?

5. **Rollout Readiness**: Are we ready to move forward with Rollout now, or do we need to strengthen our foundation first? If we're not quite ready, what specific actions will we take in the next 30–60 days to get there?

5

PLANNING YOUR ROLLOUT

If we fail to prepare, we prepare to fail.

—James H. Hope

N ow that you've assessed your readiness and committed to moving forward, it's time to create a Rollout Plan that fits your unique company. This isn't about following a rigid template or creating complex project management systems (please, no more Gantt charts!); it's about developing a thoughtful approach that considers your company's culture, size, and circumstances.

Before diving into your planning, **you may want to read the rest of this book, then return to this chapter**. Understanding all the tools, potential challenges, and success strategies covered in later chapters will help you create a more informed and realistic plan for your specific situation.

WHY PLANNING MATTERS

You wouldn't build a house without blueprints or take a cross-country road trip without a map. Yet many leadership teams approach Rollout as if they can figure it out as they go.

Companies that plan their Rollout approach have significantly higher success rates. Planning helps you avoid overwhelming your team, sequence things logically, identify potential obstacles, assign clear ownership, set realistic timelines, and maintain momentum through challenges.

Think of this as "planned spontaneity"—you want a solid plan to guide your decisions and keep you moving forward, but you also want to stay flexible and responsive to what you learn along the way. The best Rollout Plans provide structure and direction while leaving room to adjust based on what's actually working (or not working) in your specific environment.

The companies that succeed with Rollout don't just wing it. They take time to plan their approach, involve the right people, and build in flexibility for learning and adjustment along the way.

WHAT THE HECK IS A DEPARTMENT?

Before we explore how to design your Rollout approach, let's clarify what we mean by "departments," since this will be central to your planning decisions. In EOS terms, a department is a group of people who regularly work together and share responsibilities, goals, or functions.

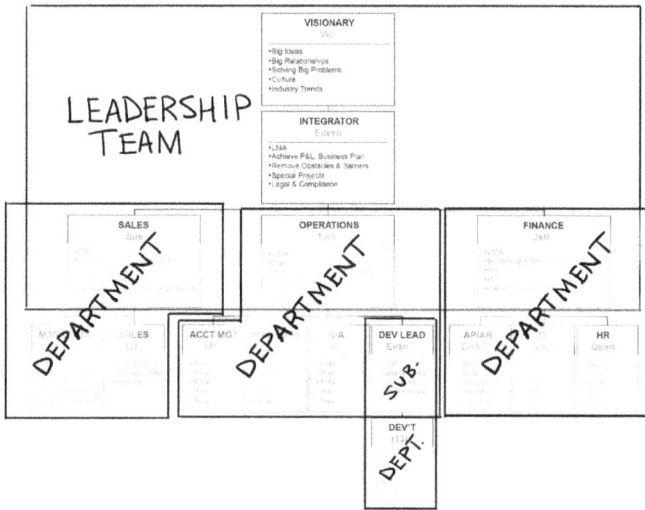

Looking at your Accountability Chart, departments typically form around the major functional areas. For example:

- **Sales and Marketing**—people focused on generating and converting leads
- **Operations**—people involved in delivering your product or service
- **Finance and Administration**—people handling financial management and support functions

That said, you may also have teams organized by division or location that could benefit from a similar "departmental" approach.

Depending on the size of your company, you may have additional teams (sub-departments) underneath these teams. For example, the Operations Department might consist of three sub-departments: Engineering, Project Management, and Manufacturing.

Now that you understand how to identify your departments, let's explore how to design a Rollout approach tailored to your specific organizational structure.

📝 **Rollout Planning Tip:** *Decide whether it makes sense to Rollout to all departments simultaneously, one department at a time, or use a different approach.*

THE FOUR PLANNING ESSENTIALS

Successful Rollout planning requires attention to four key areas that will determine whether your Rollout creates lasting change or becomes another forgotten initiative.

1. **Define Your Approach and Timeline:** Create a phased rollout that matches your company's capacity for change.

2. **Clarify Roles and Responsibilities:** Assign clear ownership and involve the right people at the right times.

3. **Plan Your Communication:** Develop messages that build excitement and address potential resistance to change.

4. **Keep It Simple and Flexible:** Try not to overcomplicate things with elaborate spreadsheets or Gantt charts. Adapt your plan as you learn what works best for your team

1. DEFINE YOUR APPROACH AND TIMELINE

Rather than trying to do everything at once (which usually ends in chaos and frustrated people), most companies benefit from introducing EOS in phases.

Consider your company's size as one factor in defining your approach, but don't let it lock you into a rigid formula. Some smaller companies (10–25 people) find it natural to introduce their vision and EOS to everyone at once while gradually rolling out tools. For example, one wealth management firm (12 people) held a single all-hands meeting to share their complete V/TO, then spent the next three months teaching one EOS Tool per month. Since everyone could fit around one conference table, they continued to hold leadership team Level 10 Meetings with three senior leaders, and started company-wide Level 10 Meetings with the whole team.

Companies with 25–100 people often find success starting with managers before expanding to frontline teams, but we've seen other organizations launch to everyone with a kick-off meeting, then use a department-by-department approach. Larger companies (100+ people) may benefit from introducing the vision and EOS to a single division or location first, but some prefer a coordinated company-wide launch.

While every company's path is different, many find success with a progression that starts with leadership mastery, then engages mid-managers as champions, and gradually expands to departments and individuals.

Your phases might look completely different based on your unique situation—and that's perfectly fine. The goal isn't to follow someone else's playbook; it's to create an approach that actually works for your team.

TIMELINE REALITY CHECK

Most leadership teams underestimate rollout time by 50 percent. Here's what typically influences your timeline.

What Accelerates Rollout: Your timeline will move faster when the leadership team models EOS consistently and mid-managers readily embrace change. Companies with existing meeting discipline and strong culture typically see quicker adoption because people are already used to structured processes. Clear consequences for non-participation and a history of successful change initiatives also help teams understand that this isn't just another passing fad.

What Slows Things Down: Expect longer timelines if you have a history of failed change initiatives, remote or multi-location teams that make consistent communication challenging, or high turnover during the rollout period. Change-resistant cultures and competing priorities or major business disruptions will also extend your journey.

Companies with fewer than 25 employees often have unique advantages in rollout—everyone knows each other, communication is faster, and changes can be implemented more quickly. However, you may need to adapt some tools: your "departments" might be project teams or functional groups rather than traditional departments, and your entire company might meet together rather than in separate departmental Level 10 Meetings. The principles remain the same; the application just scales down.

Keep these timeline principles in mind as we explore launch strategies in Chapter 6 and departmental implementation approaches in Chapter 7—rushing either phase to meet unrealistic expectations typically backfires.

CREATE YOUR ROLLOUT TIMELINE

Develop a timeline that works for your organization, considering:

- Key meetings and milestones that make sense for your company

- Training sessions for different groups
- Communication points to keep everyone informed
- Regular check-ins to assess progress and make adjustments

Remember to build in flexibility—your initial plan won't be perfect, and that's completely normal. It's better to plan conservatively and finish early than to rush the process and create resistance or poor habits that take months to correct.

Rollout Planning Tip: Build in more time than you think you'll need for each phase. Rollout can take longer than expected, and rushing can create chaos and resistance.

2. CLARIFY ROLES AND RESPONSIBILITIES

Without clear ownership, even well-intentioned Rollouts tend to lose momentum and drift off course. Identifying and clarifying who's responsible for what will ensure that you aren't stepping on each other or dropping the ball.

DESIGNATE A ROLLOUT CHAMPION

As we mentioned previously, while the entire leadership team must be actively engaged in planning your Rollout, it's generally more effective if one person owns the rollout process and keeps it moving forward. Think about who in your company naturally champions new initiatives and has the credibility to drive change.

While the Integrator often fills this role naturally, it might also be someone who's passionate about EOS, comfortable with facilitation, or detail-oriented— like your Operations Leader. The most important qualities are a genuine belief in what you're building and respect from their colleagues. Sometimes the best champions aren't the obvious choices.

INVOLVE YOUR MID-MANAGERS

While your Rollout Champion drives the process, successful Rollout planning requires active participation from the entire leadership team and strategic engagement of your mid-managers. These managers are the crucial bridge between leadership vision and frontline execution. They'll either carry the message down effectively or become bottlenecks that slow progress. That's why you need to include them in your Rollout planning as champions rather than passive participants—their buy-in and capability will determine much of your success.

We'll explore specific strategies for preparing and engaging these critical leaders in Chapter 6 when we discuss launching your Rollout, and dive deep into their role in departmental implementation in Chapter 7.

Rollout Planning Tip: Include mid-managers in your Rollout planning discussions. Their insights about team dynamics, communication preferences, and capacity for change will make your plan more realistic and effective.

3. PLAN YOUR COMMUNICATION

Before you start, align on core messages that address your team's likely questions:

- **Why are we implementing EOS?** What problem are we solving, and how will this help?

- **What does this mean for me?** How will my daily work change, and what's expected of me?

- **When will this happen?** What's the timeline, and what can I expect in the coming weeks and months?

- **Who can I ask for help?** Where do I go with questions or concerns?

- **What if I don't understand or agree?** How can I voice my concerns and get clarity?

Plan both formal communications (meetings, written updates) and informal reinforcement (daily conversations, visual reminders).

Create consistent talking points that all leaders can use when discussing the rollout. This prevents mixed messages and ensures everyone hears the same explanation of why EOS matters and how it will benefit them.

PREPARING FOR RESISTANCE

Beyond clarifying your core messages, you also need to prepare for the resistance that naturally emerges during any significant change.

Before introducing EOS, you need to acknowledge the organizational fatigue and skepticism that exists from past failed initiatives. Many team members carry what could be described as "initiative PTSD"—a wariness born from experiencing multiple programs that promised transformation but ultimately faded away. You need to take accountability for this history and validate these concerns rather than dismissing them.

Other common sources of resistance include fear of change, confusion about roles, and concern about increased workload. Develop responses to questions you're likely to hear:

- "Is this just another flavor of the month?"
- "Why should we believe this will be different?"
- "Don't we already have enough on our plates?"
- "What happens if we don't get on board?"

Address resistance by first acknowledging past disappointments and your role in them—explain that skepticism is both understandable and valuable. Share the "why" behind EOS repeatedly, provide concrete examples of benefits, give people time to express concerns and ask questions, and demonstrate your commitment through consistent follow-through.

Remember that resistance often provides valuable information about pace, support needs, or communication gaps rather than fundamental opposition to improvement. When team members push back, they're frequently signaling legitimate concerns based on past experiences rather than simply being difficult. View this feedback as an opportunity to rebuild trust and demonstrate that this implementation will be different.

Rollout Planning Tip: *Remember what we learned in Chapter 3 about the power of repetition—people need to hear your messages at least seven times before they really sink in. Build this repetition into your communication plan from the beginning, not as an afterthought when you realize people "didn't get it" the first time.*

4. KEEP IT SIMPLE AND FLEXIBLE

Try not to over-engineer your Rollout with complex tracking systems and rigid processes. Keep it simple, and be ready to adapt your plan as you learn.

The best Rollout Plans focus on:

- **Who** needs to be involved at each phase
- **What** tools will be introduced when
- **When** key meetings and milestones will occur
- **How** you'll measure progress
- **Why** each phase matters

Trust your leaders to develop their own approaches for making EOS stick in their areas. The people closest to the work often have the best insights into what will resonate with their teams.

Your Rollout Plan should evolve based on what you learn. Build in regular opportunities to gather feedback from participants, identify what's working well, and share best practices across departments. Don't forget to celebrate successes and milestones along the way—people need to see progress to maintain momentum. Most importantly, stay open to refining your approach in future phases based on real experience rather than rigidly sticking to your original plan.

YOUR ROLLOUT PLAN IS UNIQUE

The most important thing to remember is that your Rollout Plan should be uniquely yours. Use these guidelines as a starting point, but adapt everything to fit your company's culture, capacity, and circumstances. The best plan is the one your team will actually execute consistently, not the one that looks perfect on paper (or wins awards for complexity).

Take time as a leadership team to discuss these concepts, gather input from your managers, and create an approach that feels right for your company. Trust yourselves to know what will work best in your environment—you understand your company better than anyone else.

⚒ *Rollout Tool: Before moving to LAUNCH, return to the PREPARATION section of your Rollout Tracker from Chapter 1. Are you truly ready to launch your Rollout?*

CHAPTER 5 SUMMARY

Planning your EOS Rollout is essential for success, but your plan should be uniquely tailored to your company's size, culture, and circumstances. Think "planned spontaneity"—create a solid structure to guide your decisions while staying flexible enough to adjust based on what you learn along the way.

The Four Planning Essentials provide a framework for Rollout success:

1. **Define Your Approach and Timeline** by creating phases that align with your company's capacity for change, whether rolling out simultaneously to small teams or sequentially across larger organizations.

2. **Clarify Roles and Responsibilities** by designating an Internal Champion while actively engaging the leadership team and mid-managers as advocates rather than passive participants.

3. **Plan Your Communication** by developing consistent messages that proactively address concerns and potential resistance, while building in the repetition people need to absorb change.

4. **Keep It Simple and Flexible** by avoiding over-engineered systems and trusting your leaders to adapt EOS principles to their unique team dynamics.

Remember that the best plan is the one your team will actually execute consistently. Keep it simple, focus on what matters most, and build in regular opportunities to gather feedback, celebrate successes, and refine your approach based on real experience.

With your Rollout Plan in hand, you're ready for one of the most significant moments in your EOS journey: introducing your vision and EOS to your entire organization. This launch phase sets the tone for everything that follows. How you present these concepts, the energy you bring, and the context you provide will either create momentum and excitement or confusion and resistance. The goal isn't just to share information; it's to invite everyone into a shared future that they want to help create.

What's Next: In Chapter 6, we'll explore how to launch your Rollout effectively by involving your entire team, creating compelling context, and generating enthusiasm for the journey ahead.

REFLECTION QUESTIONS

1. **Define Your Approach and Timeline**: Given our company's size, culture, and complexity, should we roll out by department, by tool, or use a hybrid approach?

2. **Clarify Roles and Responsibilities**: Who in our company would be the best internal Rollout Champion? How can we ensure our leadership team and mid-managers are actively engaged in the process?

3. **Plan Your Communication**: What are the biggest concerns or questions our team members are likely to have about our vision and EOS? How can we address these proactively in our communication plan and build in the repetition people need to truly absorb these concepts?

4. **Keep it Simple and Flexible**: How will we stay open to changing our approach based on what we learn?

INTRODUCING YOUR VISION AND EOS

If you can't beat the fear, just do it scared.

—Glennon Doyle

Now that the leadership team has mastered the EOS Foundational Tools, assessed your readiness, and created a thoughtful Rollout Plan, it's time for the big reveal: telling the rest of your company where you're going and how you're going to get there. In other words, you're about to launch your Rollout by introducing your vision and EOS to your entire team. This is when your EOS Rollout truly begins.

If you're feeling a mix of excitement and anxiety about this moment, you're in excellent company. It's completely normal to wonder how people will react when you introduce the vision and EOS to the rest of the organization. Maybe you're worried about resistance to learning something new, or perhaps you're hesitant to share information you've kept close to the vest until now.

Our experience with Rollouts has taught us that as people see EOS delivering real results and creating genuine improvements in how work gets done, they will get on board. In fact, some of the most cautious skeptics often become the biggest EOS cheerleaders once they experience its power first-hand. There's nothing quite like a reformed cynic to spread the word about something that actually works.

Don't let these understandable worries hold you back from getting what you want from your business. Remember, if you want to achieve your vision, you need to eventually roll out all five EOS Foundational Tools to the entire company: V/TO, The Accountability Chart, Rocks, The Meeting Pulse, and Scorecard.

The keyword here is **EVENTUALLY**. Even if you're not ready to roll out all five Foundational Tools right now, you can still begin your Rollout journey. You don't have to be perfect; you simply have to start.

FIVE BEST PRACTICES FOR A SUCCESSFUL LAUNCH

You know your team, culture, and circumstances better than anyone, which means there's no one-size-fits-all approach to introducing the vision and EOS. You could schedule an all-hands kickoff meeting to create excitement and momentum. You might prefer to meet in smaller teams or groups for more intimate conversations. In smaller companies, leaders might choose to sit down one-on-one with each employee for personalized discussions.

You can introduce all the tools at once if your team handles change well, or teach them one at a time over several months if a gradual approach feels more sustainable. You might share the entire V/TO in one sitting for maximum impact, or introduce it section by section to allow for deeper absorption and discussion.

The possibilities are endless, but these five best practices consistently lead to successful launches:

1. **Involve the entire leadership team** to demonstrate unity and shared commitment.

2. **Prepare your mid-managers** as champions and bridges to their teams.

3. **Create context for the content** so people understand the "why" behind each tool.

4. **Make it visible** through multiple channels and creative reinforcement.

5. **Repeat yourself often** (at least 7 times!) to ensure understanding and retention.

Let's explore each of these elements in detail.

1. INVOLVE THE ENTIRE LEADERSHIP TEAM

It's natural to think the Visionary or Owner should launch your Rollout, but we've found that launches are more effective when the entire leadership team is actively involved in introducing the vision and EOS to the entire company. In addition to presenting a united front, each leader will develop the skills they need to champion the Rollout in their own departments.

Every member of the leadership team should be able to:

- Give a compelling high-level overview of EOS and why you chose it

- Introduce each EOS Foundational Tool with appropriate context and enthusiasm

- Communicate the vision consistently using the same language and stories

- Answer common questions about how EOS will affect daily work
- Address resistance or concerns with empathy and clarity

Think of your launch as the leadership team's debut performance. Everyone needs to know their role and understand how they contribute to the overall success of the production.

Rollout Planning Tip: If you're planning a kickoff meeting or presentation, consider practicing together as a leadership team. You'd be surprised how often rehearsal reveals gaps in understanding and alignment.

REAL-WORLD SUCCESS STORY: THE POWER OF UNITY

Campus Cooks, a kitchen management company with locations across the United States, faced a common Rollout challenge: how do you introduce EOS to managers scattered across multiple states? Their solution was both practical and powerful.

The timing couldn't have been better. Just after completing Vision Building Day 2, Campus Cooks had their annual management meeting scheduled—a three-day event that would bring together all regional and senior managers in one place. Visionary Bill Reeder and Integrator Joe Nelson saw the perfect opportunity to launch their rollout with maximum impact.

Rather than having one person present the entire vision, Bill and Joe strategically divided the presentation. Bill took the Vision side of the V/TO, walking through their Core Values, Core Focus, 10-Year Target, Marketing Strategy, and 3-Year Picture with genuine passion and conviction. Then Joe brought the vision down to earth, explaining the practical 1-Year Plan, current Rocks, and Issues List with equal enthusiasm. Finally, the entire leadership team participated in the Q&A session, exemplifying a united commitment to the vision and EOS.

"The energy in the room was electric," Bill recalled. What made the difference wasn't just the content; it was the obvious unity between Bill and Joe. They finished each other's sentences, built on each other's points, and demonstrated the kind of alignment they were asking their managers to embrace.

"Employees later told us they'd never seen us so aligned and enthusiastic about anything," Joe reflected. "That unified presentation convinced even our most skeptical team members that this wasn't just another passing fad."

Six months later, their rollout was ahead of schedule across all locations. When asked what made the difference, both Bill and Joe pointed back to that launch meeting. "We proved that we were truly united around this vision before we asked anyone else to buy in," Bill said. "That authenticity made all the difference."

2. PREPARE YOUR MID-MANAGERS

In *Traction*, Gino Wickman recommends rolling the tools out one tier at a time, starting with the people who report to the leadership team.[3] In some companies, everyone reports directly to the leadership team. In larger organizations, there's usually a group of "mid-managers" who report to leadership and manage their own teams. Looking at your Accountability Chart, these seats should have LMA (Leadership, Management, and Accountability) listed as their first role, because they are responsible for leading and managing their team.

In companies with fewer than 25 people, you may not have traditional mid-managers. In these cases, consider identifying informal influencers or your most experienced team members to help champion the Rollout alongside the leadership team.

These are the people who will make or break your Rollout. They're the bridge between leadership vision and frontline execution. They either carry the message down or drop it. They either reinforce the tools daily or quietly resist them. They translate your passion into practical application or let it die in the chaos of daily operations.

If mid-managers aren't intentionally included in your Rollout strategy, they'll either:

1. **Create invisible friction** by passively resisting or inconsistently implementing
2. **Fade into dangerous invisibility** by neither supporting nor opposing the rollout

Neither scenario leads to success. These managers need to become active advocates, not passive participants.

To help your mid-managers understand what's coming, it's a good idea to introduce them to the EOS Foundational Tools before rolling out EOS to the broader team. This approach provides several benefits:

- **Processing Time:** They have dedicated time to understand concepts without the pressure to teach them immediately.
- **Space to Question:** They can ask questions they might not feel comfortable asking in front of their teams.

- **Skill and Confidence Building:** They begin building fluency in the system before needing to demonstrate competence.

- **Voice and Input:** They feel included in the planning rather than just told what to implement.

As we discussed in Chapter 5's planning framework, identifying and preparing these managers is crucial to the success of the Rollout. The investment you make in these managers during launch will pay dividends when they begin implementing departmental EOS practices, which we'll cover in detail in Chapter 7.

While strong communication is essential, larger organizations often benefit from additional support structures to maintain consistency and momentum across multiple departments.

REAL-WORLD EXAMPLE: THE EOS CHAMPIONS NETWORK

When UCP, a large Hong Kong-based company with hundreds of employees, began their Rollout, they faced two significant challenges: maintaining consistency across a large workforce and the fact that while leadership implemented EOS in English, hundreds of frontline employees were not fluent in English.

Their solution was both practical and powerful: create an **EOS Champions Network**—a team of volunteers who genuinely loved EOS and wanted to help spread it throughout the organization.

Rather than placing the entire rollout burden on leadership, UCP identified employees at various levels who had caught the EOS vision early and were naturally enthusiastic. These weren't necessarily the most senior people; they were simply people who "got it" and wanted others to benefit from what they were learning.

Working collaboratively with the Integrator, the Champions team translated EOS Tools into Chinese while ensuring core concepts remained intact, developed relatable examples that connected to local culture and daily work experiences, and created peer-learning opportunities where they could demonstrate the tools in employees' native language.

This grassroots approach created unexpected benefits. When peers taught peers, resistance decreased. The Champions heard concerns that never made it to leadership meetings, allowing proactive problem-solving. Instead of having one Rollout Champion as the single point of knowledge, multiple people across the organization could answer questions and provide guidance.

"The Champions didn't just translate words; they translated concepts into culturally relevant examples that resonated more deeply than any imported case studies could," reflected their Integrator. "They made EOS feel accessible and relevant to everyone, not just those comfortable with English or Western business frameworks."

Rollout Planning Tip: *For organizations with 100+ employees or multiple locations, consider whether a group like this EOS Champions Network, might accelerate your Rollout while creating stronger cultural adoption. The investment in developing these internal advocates often pays dividends in faster, more sustainable implementation.*

3. CREATE CONTEXT FOR THE CONTENT

Whether you're introducing only your V/TO or all five EOS Foundational Tools at once, sharing content without context is like handing someone a map without telling them where they are or where they're trying to go. Content without context will create confusion, and confusion kills momentum.

REAL-WORLD EXAMPLE: THE DISASTER OF CONTENT WITHOUT CONTEXT

A successful landscaping company owner learned this lesson the hard way during her EOS kickoff meeting. Excited to share her newly completed vision and organizational structure, she distributed copies of the V/TO and The Accountability Chart to her 15-person team without any preparation or explanation.

The disaster unfolded in real time. As team members reviewed The Accountability Chart, several people discovered their roles had fundamentally changed: some were now reporting to different managers, others had gained or lost responsibilities, and a few found themselves in completely new positions. Worst of all, no one had been given advance notice or context about these changes.

The results were immediate and devastating.

- Two valued employees quit on the spot, feeling blindsided and disrespected.

- Others became defensive and angry about their new reporting relationships.

- Questions flooded in about why these changes were necessary.

- Team members who weren't directly affected became worried about future surprises.

- The entire team developed a negative association with EOS before they even understood what it was.

The recovery took months of rebuilding trust and having the difficult conversations that should have happened before the meeting. The owner later reflected, "Now whenever we mention EOS, some people still remember that awful meeting. I was so focused on sharing our new direction that I forgot these changes would affect real people's lives. I should have created a communication plan that took these factors into account before revealing everything publicly."

CREATING CONTEXT FOR EOS

To avoid this kind of confusion, it's helpful to share a high-level overview of EOS before diving into the content of your Foundational Tools. Some teams verbally explain this context, others share YouTube videos or create a PowerPoint, and most hand out a copy of *What the Heck is EOS?*, written specifically for employees of companies running on EOS, to help them understand the basics.[4]

What is EOS, and Why Did You Choose It?

- Brief explanation of EOS as a complete system for organizational clarity and alignment
- The specific problems it's designed to solve (that your organization has been experiencing)
- Why you believe it's the right solution for your company's next level of growth

The EOS Model and the Journey to 80+ Percent Strong

- Overview of the Six Key Components and what "strong" looks like in each area
- Explanation that this is a journey, not a destination, with continuous improvement
- Realistic timeline expectations for seeing meaningful results

The EOS Foundational Tools—How Each Tool Is Used

- High-level preview of the five tools they'll be learning
- Brief explanation of how each tool strengthens specific components
- Assurance that they'll receive proper training and support for each tool

Every company finds their own path to a successful launch. Here are three examples that show how different organizations adapted these principles to their unique situations:

Silverlake Design and Marketing (10 people) started their Rollout with a company potluck. Everyone had read *What the Heck is EOS?* beforehand, so the leadership team could dive straight into reviewing their V/TO and The Accountability Chart, along with the Rocks they had set for the quarter. They also taught the Level 10 Meeting Agenda and introduced the concept of Scorecards. Because they are a marketing company, they redesigned their EOS documents with their own branding, turning the rollout preparation into a creative project that got their designers excited about the content. Simple and effective.

Four Seasons Kanga Roof (60 people) scheduled two separate kickoff meetings: one for the office staff and one for the field crew, recognizing that these groups had different schedules and communication preferences. They gave a high-level overview of EOS, shared their Core Values, and handed out copies of *What the Heck is EOS?*. "We knew our team would be overwhelmed if we shared everything at once," said Visionary Bill Burkhardt, Sr. "A phased approach made more sense—introducing the vision piece by piece." Over the next couple of months, they repeated these meetings and shared a few more sections of the V/TO, allowing people time to absorb each concept before adding the next.

Skidmore Sales and Distributing Co. (260 people) faced a unique challenge: rolling out EOS across four different subsidiaries with vastly different sizes and focuses. Doug Skidmore, the Visionary/Owner, attended independent rollout meetings at each subsidiary rather than attempting a one-size-fits-all approach. Each subsidiary's Integrator designed their own kickoff meeting, tailoring the format to their team size—from formal presentations for 150+ employees to intimate conversations for smaller teams. "We learned that consistency in vision doesn't require identical implementation," Doug reflected.

✎ *Mastery Tip: Use existing resources from EOS Worldwide to educate your team.*

- *What the Heck is EOS?*—a book written specifically for employees to help them understand key concepts and how the EOS Foundational Tools work; visit TractionLibrary. com to learn more and purchase copies for your team.
- *You can find links to other EOS Worldwide resources in the Resource Center on our website, RolloutBook.com.*

CREATING CONTEXT FOR YOUR VISION

When you're ready to share your V/TO, it's crucial to "tee up" each section with talking points that explain the purpose of each section and how it will be used going forward. Think of yourself as a tour guide introducing each landmark and explaining its significance.

CONTEXT + CONTENT = 💡

For example, when sharing Core Values, you might say: "Core Values define who we are as a company and the culture we're committed to building together. These aren't just nice words on a poster; they're the standards we'll use to hire new people, make decisions about promotions, recognize great performance, and, when necessary, help people who aren't a cultural fit find a better situation. We want every single person here to live and breathe these values every day because they represent the kind of workplace we all want to be part of."

You don't have to use these exact words, but it's crucial that the leadership team agrees on the language you'll use to create context and explain each section of the V/TO. "Winging it" will only create confusion if different leaders are using different language to explain the same concepts. After this setup, you'd deliver your Core Values Speech, walking through each value and explaining what it means in practical, everyday terms.

Consistency is key—your vision should sound the same whether it comes from the Visionary, the department manager, or any other leader in the organization.

Rollout Planning Tip: Think through the top questions your team is likely to ask and either address concerns proactively or prepare answers so you don't inadvertently cause confusion.

SAMPLE V/TO TALKING POINTS TO CREATE CONTEXT

Core Values:

- Who we are as people and as a company
- They define our culture and guide our behavior
- Used to hire, fire, review, reward, and recognize team members

Core Focus:

- Why we exist and what we do best
- Our sweet spot in the marketplace
- Internal decision-making filter that helps us avoid "shiny stuff" or distractions

10-Year Target/Core Target:

- Where we're going as an organization
- Big, long-range energizing goal that gets everyone excited
- The achievement we'll celebrate together when we reach it

Marketing Strategy:

- How we're going to reach our 10-Year Target and grow the business
- Focuses our sales and marketing energy on the right activities

- ○ Target Market—our ideal customer/who we serve best
- ○ 3 Uniques—what differentiates us from the competition
- ○ Proven Process—how we consistently deliver value; how we set, manage, and deliver on expectations
- ○ Guarantee—how we give customers confidence

3-Year Picture:

- What success looks like three years from now
- Specific, measurable progress toward our 10-Year Target
- Close your eyes and picture the future

1-Year Plan:

- What we're focused on achieving this year
- Our priorities for the next 12 months
- Annual goals that move us toward the 3-Year Picture

Rocks:

- Our 90-Day Priorities as a company
- What we're focused on completing in the next quarter
- The most important things that can't wait

Issues List:

- Our parking lot
- Issues we know need attention but aren't our current focus
- Problems we're committed to solving systematically

REAL-WORLD EXAMPLE: CONSISTENCY IN ACTION

Total Security Solutions, a 120+-person manufacturing company, provides each leader and manager with an outline of talking points for each section of the V/TO. In addition to context-setting language, they include content talking points (how to discuss the 10-Year Target, what to emphasize, questions to ask the team to encourage discussion, etc.) to ensure everyone communicates the vision clearly and consistently.

"We can't build a strong culture if everyone's hearing different messages from different leaders," explains Christine Sermak, Chief People Officer. "The talking points aren't about making people sound like robots; they're about making sure the foundation is solid so leaders can add their own flavor on top. When everyone knows we're all saying the same thing about what matters most, trust goes way up."

Each leader injects their own stories and examples to connect the dots for their team, but the key messages and themes are the same. This investment in consistency pays off dramatically—employees report that they're always clear about the company's direction, regardless of which leader they're talking with.

CREATING CONTEXT FOR YOUR OTHER FOUNDATIONAL TOOLS

Each tool has the potential to trigger resistance if mishandled during initial introduction. Here's how to frame each tool to maximize adoption and minimize defensive reactions:

THE ACCOUNTABILITY CHART

When introducing The Accountability Chart, simply explain that it shows who reports to whom and who is accountable for what. Most organizations struggle with unclear responsibilities, and this tool finally provides the clarity everyone has been desperately seeking.

Highlight that functions—not titles—appear at the top of each seat, reinforcing that what you do matters more than what you're called. Keep the five roles in each seat focused on broad accountabilities rather than granular tasks. Think "vendor relationships" instead of "review vendor contracts monthly."

This approach prevents The Accountability Chart from becoming a micromanagement tool while ensuring everyone knows exactly where to go with questions or issues. Help people see that this eliminates those frustrating "who handles this?" conversations that waste everyone's time—when you need something or have a question, you'll know exactly who to talk to.

ROCKS

When introducing the concept of Rocks, explain that they are simply the most important things to get done in the next ninety days.

Emphasize that Rocks are not "extra" work. Instead, help your team see how completing each Rock will solve the recurring issues that currently drain their time and energy, or highlight the benefits they'll experience once the Rock is accomplished.

For example, the customer database cleanup Rock isn't just busywork; it's the key to reliable data that helps salespeople track their closing rates and maximize their commissions. The process improvement Rock eliminates the manual workarounds that waste everyone's time. The training Rock gives people skills that advance their careers.

This shift in perspective transforms Rocks from burdensome obligations into welcome opportunities for meaningful progress.

THE MEETING PULSE

When introducing The Meeting Pulse, try using an EKG metaphor—meetings are your organization's heartbeat. Most teams operate with an irregular cadence—either disconnected circles where issues fester unresolved, or overlapping circles that lead to micromanagement and hinder autonomy. The healthy heartbeat occurs when circles connect just enough to stay aligned, then separate to allow independent execution.

1. DISCONNECTED
   • NOT ON THE SAME PAGE

2. SMOTHERING
   • YOU'RE MICRO-MANAGING

3. IDEAL
   • KEEPING CONNECTED

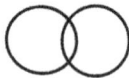

Task-driven team members often view regular meetings as interruptions to "real work." Help them understand the true cost of misalignment by sharing concrete examples: the project that went sideways because assumptions weren't clarified, the client issue that escalated because the right hand didn't know what the left was doing, or the duplicate efforts that wasted hours because communication happened through a game of telephone.

Investing focused time in meetings prevents scattered interruptions, emergency fire drills, and cleanup efforts that consume far more time when teams aren't meeting regularly. This is an investment in their autonomy—the better aligned everyone is going into the week, quarter, and year, the more independently everyone can operate.

SCORECARD

When introducing the concept of a Scorecard, it can be helpful to present it as a success-tracking system rather than a surveillance tool. Address the micromanagement concern head-on by emphasizing that Scorecards create transparency that actually reduces oversight. When everyone can see the numbers, there's less need for check-ins, status updates, and progress reports.

Accountable people love to be held accountable. High performers naturally gravitate toward accountability because it validates their contributions and provides objective recognition for their efforts. The key is to position Scorecard Measurables as a way to both celebrate success and smoke out issues when things are off track.

You might explain it this way: when you hit your numbers, you know you're winning before anyone else tells you. This shifts the energy from defensive to proactive—from "Am I in trouble?" to "How can I stay on track?" This creates confidence rather than anxiety about performance expectations.

4. MAKE IT VISIBLE

To make the vision and EOS more compelling and memorable, consider using visuals to support your Rollout. From presentations to signage to swag, there are countless creative ways to get your team excited about the journey to 80+ percent strong and ensure the vision becomes part of daily conversation rather than just quarterly presentations.

CREATIVE EXAMPLES FROM REAL-WORLD COMPANIES

Branding and Swag:

- T-shirts with company's purpose on the front and core values on the back
- Coffee mugs featuring the 10-Year Target
- Mouse pads with the Proven Process steps

Physical Displays:

- Banners with 3 Uniques displayed prominently on the manufacturing floor
- Digital signage rotating through vision components in common areas
- Laminated V/TO sheets posted in break rooms, conference rooms, and yes, even bathrooms
- Whiteboards tracking the company and departmental Rock progress

Digital Integration:

- Company screensavers featuring Core Values and other V/TO elements
- Email signatures featuring the 3 Uniques
- Intranet homepage highlighting current Rocks and Scorecard results
- Video displays in lobbies showing customer success stories that illustrate the company's Core Focus

Fun and Memorable:

- Temporary tattoos featuring core values for company events (surprisingly popular!)
- Desk calendars with a monthly focus on different V/TO components
- Parking spot rewards for team members who exemplify core values

---

REAL-WORLD EXAMPLE: MAKING CORE VALUES IMPOSSIBLE TO IGNORE

When Blue Chip Partners, a 35-person wealth management firm, clarified their Core Values—We Elevate the Client Experience, We are Team Players, We Act with Integrity, We Focus on Growth, We Take Initiative, and We are Problem Solvers—they became impossible to ignore throughout the organization.

Signage hangs throughout their office, branded materials with the Core Values are distributed to every team member, and the team uses a dedicated Shout Outs channel in Microsoft Teams to recognize colleagues for demonstrating the values in action. During State of the Company meetings, several team members consistently recognize others for living the Core Values and celebrate specific examples of how people embody them. Their website's "Careers" page prominently features the Core Values, and their advisor and client services teams embody them in every client interaction.

"We keep our Core Values visible everywhere because out of sight really does mean out of mind," explains Integrator Erin Goss. "When people see them daily—on the walls, in meetings, in how we recognize each other— they naturally become part of how we think and make decisions. It's not about being preachy; it's about keeping what matters most front and center."

This comprehensive visibility has created a unified organizational identity, enabling everyone to articulate the values and reference them in daily decisions and conversations.

IMPORTANT REALITY CHECK

That said, coffee mugs and t-shirts are not a substitute for consistently walking the talk as leaders and managers. If you hand out coasters with your core values but then keep people in the organization who consistently perform below the bar or violate those values, you'll quickly find those coasters in the trash— along with your credibility.

Visual reinforcement is powerful when backed by authentic leadership behavior. When it's just decoration without substance, it becomes a source of cynicism rather than inspiration.

5. REPEAT YOURSELF OFTEN

Once you've communicated the vision to the entire company, you'll need to keep repeating it — over and over—not only to help people learn and embrace the concepts, but also to show that you're serious about creating permanent change in the organization.

Repetition drives progress on the journey to 80+ percent strong. The more progress the team sees, the more likely they'll be to embrace the vision and use of EOS tools and disciplines.

REAL-WORLD EXAMPLE: THE GARBAGE CAN TEST

One of our EOS clients learned this lesson the hard way during their company-wide Rollout kickoff meeting. This manufacturing company, with about 50 employees, gathered everyone in their large conference room for the big reveal of their newly completed V/TO. The leadership team was excited and nervous as they handed out beautifully printed copies of their vision to everyone.

The presentation went well. The leadership team explained each section of the V/TO with passion and conviction. They answered questions, provided context, and felt genuinely good about how the meeting had gone. Employees filed out through the single door leading to the shop floor, and the leadership team began cleaning up.

That's when they discovered something both heartbreaking and enlightening: next to the door sat a garbage can, and in it were all 50 copies of their V/TO. Every single one.

The Visionary's first instinct was discouragement. "Maybe our vision isn't compelling enough," he worried.

"Maybe our people don't care about where we're going as a company."

Then he remembered what his EOS Implementer had told him: "Don't expect your people to pick you up and put you on their shoulders and cheer you out the door the first time you share this. Expect folded arms, doubt, and resistance. They need to hear it seven times before it really sinks in."

So they didn't give up. The next quarter, they held another State of the Company meeting and shared the V/TO again. This time, fewer copies ended up in the garbage can, but still quite a few. The quarter after that, even fewer. Each time they shared their vision, more people held onto their copies, asked better questions, and seemed more engaged with the content.

By the seventh time they presented their V/TO, the garbage can remained empty. More importantly, employees were asking how their specific work connected to the 10-Year Target, referencing core values in daily conversations, and demonstrating genuine ownership of the company's direction.

"The garbage can test taught us that persistence pays off," the Visionary reflected years later. "Our people weren't rejecting our vision; they simply needed time to understand it was real and wasn't going away. Now they're some of our biggest champions for what we're building together."

This story illustrates a crucial truth about rollout: initial resistance doesn't mean your vision is wrong or your people don't care. It usually means they're protecting themselves from getting excited about another initiative that might disappear in a few months. Your job is to prove through consistent repetition that this time is different.

STATE OF THE COMPANY MEETINGS

Embracing the discipline of a Quarterly State of the Company meeting will ensure your team hears the vision at least every ninety days while celebrating progress and realigning on priorities for the next quarter.

State of the Company meetings are typically short (less than 45 minutes) and follow a simple format:

- **Where you've been**—what you accomplished last quarter: Rocks, numbers, new customers, wins worth celebrating
- **Where you are**—current initiatives, work anniversaries, team updates
- **Where you're going**—Core Values, Core Focus, 10-Year Target, Marketing Strategy, 3-Year Picture, 1-Year Plan, next quarter Rocks, Long-Term Issues

Each quarter, the leadership team should create an agenda following this format, filling in each section with the information you want to convey to the entire company. As with the launch, it's smart to involve the entire leadership team in the State of the Company presentation to maintain a united front.

REAL-WORLD EXAMPLES: STATE OF THE COMPANY

In-Person State of the Company: Clear Height Properties' State of the Company meetings have evolved significantly over their eight-year EOS journey. What started as straightforward quarterly updates has become engaging celebrations that reflect their core value of "have fun and excitement every day" while driving results.

Each meeting begins with an inclusion exercise—perhaps a scavenger hunt or a "Guess the Number" game tied to their financial literacy training. This isn't just ice-breaking; it's intentional culture-building that gets everyone engaged before diving into business content.

After the team has had some fun, they review the V/TO and discuss the previous quarter's performance. The highlight is the Core Values Awards, where team members are recognized for exemplifying the company's values in practice. Clear Height has also gamified Rock completion, creating friendly competition between departments for the highest completion score—turning accountability into motivation.

The meeting, however, doesn't end when the formal agenda concludes. The entire team participates in a group activity afterward: tailgating in the company parking lot, bowling, TopGolf, or dinner at a local Mexican restaurant. These activities reinforce that Clear Height isn't just talking about having fun as a core value; they're living it consistently.

"The evolution of our State of the Company meetings reflects our growth as an organization and embodies who we are at our core," explains Dominic Sergi, Visionary. "We've learned that when people genuinely enjoy being together, the business fulfills its Core Purpose of 'Building Wealth and Creating Legacies' not only for ourselves, but for everyone we come in contact with."

Remote State of the Company: City of Faith, a federal halfway house with three locations, has mastered the art of connecting their distributed team through their quarterly State of the Company meetings. Their Visionary and Integrator duo creates a comprehensive video presentation that covers "where we've been, where we are, and where we're going," ensuring the core message around their Vision/Traction Organizer remains consistent across all locations.

Rather than relying solely on recorded content, they take their show on the road, conducting live sessions at each of their three facilities. This hybrid approach combines the consistency of a prepared presentation with the personal connection of face-to-face interaction. During these visits, the leadership team fields questions directly from staff, creating genuine dialogue and ensuring everyone feels heard and connected to the organization's direction.

Recognizing that not everyone can attend the scheduled sessions due to varying shifts and responsibilities inherent in their 24/7 operation, the Visionary and Integrator hold dedicated office hours after each State of the Company cycle. These one-on-one or small-group sessions ensure that every team member—regardless of their schedule—has access to leadership and can get their specific questions answered.

This thoughtful approach demonstrates that intentional culture-building in a remote or multi-location environment requires both consistency in messaging and flexibility in delivery, ensuring no one is left out of the communication loop.

DEPARTMENTAL QUARTERLY AND ANNUAL MEETING PULSE

We'll dive deeper into departmental Quarterly Planning Meetings in Chapter 7, but it's worth noting here that you have another powerful opportunity to reinforce the V/TO each quarter before setting departmental Rocks.

This provides essential context and ensures that departmental Rocks align with Company Goals and Rocks—keeping everyone rowing in the same direction rather than pursuing competing priorities.

During these meetings, department leaders can:

- Review relevant sections of the V/TO and connect them to departmental work
- Share stories about how the department is living the Core Values
- Explain how departmental goals support the 3-Year Picture and 1-Year Plan
- Set departmental Rocks that clearly connect to company priorities
- Address questions or concerns specific to that department's role

TAKING IT TO THE NEXT LEVEL

Once you have successfully launched your Rollout by introducing your vision and EOS company-wide, your people will understand where the company is headed, how EOS will help you get there, and what their role is in the journey. The journey continues from there: launching company-wide is just the beginning—the real transformation happens when EOS moves from the leadership team into the daily operations of each department. The next phase of your Rollout involves taking these Foundational Tools deeper into your organization, empowering your departmental leaders to create their own accountability systems, and ensuring that the EOS disciplines become embedded in how work actually gets done at every level. It's time to move from company-wide awareness to departmental mastery.

⚒ *Rollout Tool: Launch complete? Check the LAUNCH section of your Rollout Tracker to verify you haven't missed anything.*

CHAPTER 6 SUMMARY

Successfully introducing your vision and EOS means moving from leadership team mastery to company-wide understanding and buy-in. You don't need to be perfect; you simply need to start with authentic commitment and clear purpose. Expect natural skepticism from teams that have experienced "flavor-of-the-month" initiatives, but remember that even cautious skeptics often become the strongest advocates once they see real results.

Key elements of effective launches include:

- Involve the entire leadership team to demonstrate unity and shared commitment
- Prepare and engage mid-managers as champions and bridges to their teams
- Create context for content so people understand the "why" behind each tool
- Make it visible through multiple channels and creative reinforcement
- Repeat yourself often (at least 7 times!) to ensure understanding and retention

Remember that sharing content without context creates confusion, and confusion kills momentum. Each EOS tool should be introduced with clear explanations of its purpose and benefits. Visual reinforcement only works when backed by authentic leadership behavior—coffee mugs with core values become sources of cynicism if leaders don't consistently model those values.

Successfully launching company-wide awareness is simply the beginning of the Rollout journey—the real transformation happens when EOS moves from understanding to daily practice. While your team now knows where you're going and how EOS will help you get there, knowing about the tools and actually using them consistently are two very different things. The next phase of your Rollout involves taking these foundational concepts deeper into your organization, empowering your departmental leaders to create their own accountability systems, and ensuring that EOS disciplines become embedded in how work actually gets done at every level.

What's Next: In Chapter 7, we'll explore how to take your Rollout deeper into the organization by implementing departmental-level EOS practices and creating accountability systems at every level.

REFLECTION QUESTIONS

1. **Leadership team involvement**: Is our entire leadership team prepared to introduce the vision and EOS together, or are we relying too heavily on one person? What does each leader need to know and be able to explain confidently?

2. **Mid-manager preparation**: Have we identified and prepared our mid-managers to champion the Rollout? What specific support do they need to carry the message effectively to their teams?

3. **Context before content**: For each foundational tool we'll introduce, have we developed clear talking points that explain WHY it matters before diving into WHAT it is? Where might confusion arise if we skip this step?

4. **Making it visible**: Beyond the initial announcement, how will we keep the vision and EOS visible in daily work? What visual reminders or creative approaches would resonate with our team?

5. **Repetition discipline**: How will we ensure the vision gets repeated consistently—not just once, but quarter after quarter? What's our plan for regular State of the Company meetings?

7

ROLLING OUT TO DEPARTMENTS

If you want to go fast, go alone.
If you want to go far, go together.

—African Proverb

With your company-wide Launch complete, you're moving into the Integration phase—taking EOS deeper into your organization through systematic departmental implementation.

In Chapter 6, you shared the vision and introduced EOS concepts to your entire organization. Now comes the next critical phase: moving from awareness to implementation. Once you've introduced the vision and EOS to your entire team, it's time to start actively implementing EOS Foundational Tools at the departmental level.

As we discussed in Chapter 5, departments are groups of people who work together regularly and share responsibilities—typically organized around major functions like Sales, Marketing, Operations, and Finance, though they may also be organized by division or location. If you have mid-managers, they will become the key drivers of departmental success. Their understanding of EOS concepts and commitment to the vision will determine how effectively your Foundational Tools take root at the departmental level.

Just as there's no one-size-fits-all approach to introducing your vision and EOS, there's no universally "right" way to get departments using the EOS Foundational Tools effectively. Some companies roll out one tool at a time, one level at a time, while others introduce multiple tools to multiple teams simultaneously. What's essential is choosing an approach that fits your organization's size, culture, and capacity for change.

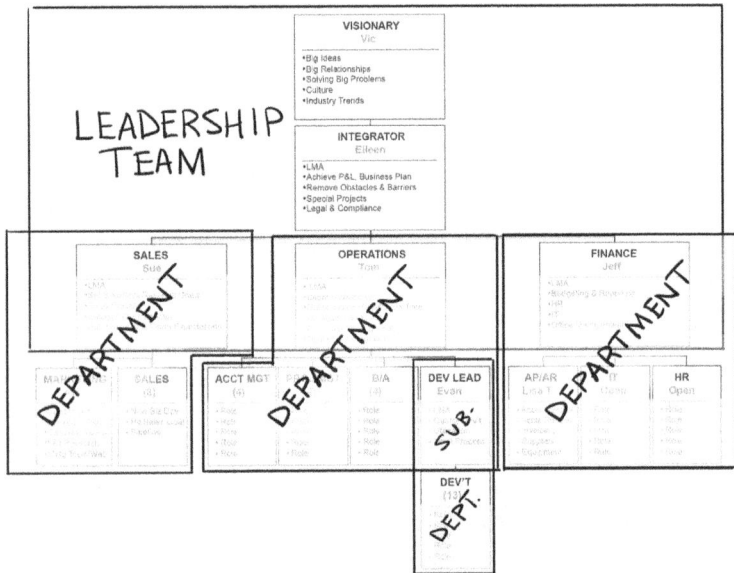

DEPARTMENTAL LEVEL 10 MEETINGS

When Level 10 Meetings are fully rolled out in Departments, each team will meet regularly following the Level 10 Meeting Agenda, which includes a review of the Scorecard and Rocks.

That said, you can still get started with holding departmental Level 10 Meetings even if you don't have a Scorecard or Rocks yet—just skip those agenda items temporarily, and add them back in when you are ready. The important thing is to develop the discipline of meeting regularly as a team to drive accountability and solve issues, and the Level 10 Meeting agenda is the most effective way to accomplish this.

Another major benefit of starting departmental Level 10 Meetings is that you can start to categorize issues more effectively—putting the right issues in front of the right people at the right time. When you first start running Level 10 Meetings as a leadership team, it's common for the issues list to be full of issues that are actually more departmental in nature. If you don't have a place to address these issues, they're going to keep bubbling up to the leadership team, which will take your time and energy away from working on higher-level issues. Not only will you get better buy-in when departmental team members are involved in solving their own issues, but you'll also free up the leadership team to focus on more important things.

Mastery Tip: For more detailed guidance on running Level 10 Meetings, see Chapter 8 of Traction *by Gino Wickman.*

MEETING FREQUENCY AND DURATION

While leadership team Level 10 Meetings are held weekly for 90 minutes, you may need to adjust the frequency and duration of departmental Level 10 Meetings to match each team's unique needs.

Finding the right Meeting Pulse for each department is like tuning an instrument—it requires experimentation and adjustment until you hit the right frequency. Most departments discover that weekly meetings create the perfect balance, maintaining alignment without overwhelming busy schedules. However, each team's needs are unique. Your sales team might find that a crisp 60-minute weekly meeting keeps deals moving and energy high, while your operations team may need the full 90 minutes to work through complex production challenges. Meanwhile, your finance team might operate effectively with bi-weekly 45-minute meetings, since their work often follows monthly cycles rather than weekly sprints.

The key is to start somewhere and stay responsive to what actually works for each team, then maintain that consistency once you find the right pulse. Your meeting pulse should be reviewed periodically to ensure it continues serving everyone effectively.

Regardless of the duration you choose, it's important to keep the Level 10 Meeting agenda structure intact. There's specific psychology and methodology built into the agenda (detailed in Chapter 8 of *Traction*) that's designed to drive accountability and help you gain traction. As long as 50 percent of the time is spent on IDS, you can adjust the meeting duration to meet your team's needs.

MEETING ATTENDEES

The most effective departmental Level 10 Meetings typically bring together people who work closely together and share accountability for results. Sometimes this means traditional functional departments like sales, operations, or finance. Other times, it makes more sense to organize around geographic divisions, especially for companies with multiple locations where regional teams face similar challenges. You might even find that cross-functional project teams need their own meeting pulse to stay aligned on complex initiatives that span multiple departments.

The guiding principle is simple: Invite active participants, not passive observers. Every person in the room should bring valuable data, possess relevant knowledge, and be able to help solve issues that arise during discussions.

In very small organizations, your "departmental" Level 10 Meeting might include the entire company. This is perfectly fine—just maintain the same agenda discipline and ensure everyone has meaningful numbers and Rocks to report on.

Department leaders should thoughtfully curate their attendee list rather than defaulting to "everyone's invited." While inclusion feels good, effective meetings require people who can meaningfully contribute to discussions and decision-making. You may need to experiment with different combinations to find the right mix—the group that can efficiently review numbers, surface real issues, and commit to solutions. This isn't about excluding people from information; it's about optimizing the meeting for results while ensuring broader communication happens through other channels.

MEETING FACILITATION

Most effective Level 10 Meetings have two key roles: a facilitator and a scribe. The facilitator follows the agenda, keeps things moving, encourages participation, and prevents the team from going off-topic. The scribe manages the "paperwork" or digital tools—adding issues and To-dos, updating Rocks and Measurables, and maintaining meeting documentation. Splitting these roles is essential because facilitating and capturing require different brain functions—when one person tries to do both, constant task-switching slows the meeting and kills momentum.

Leadership Team Member as Facilitator: Some companies start by having a leadership team member facilitate departmental Level 10 Meetings, since they have experience participating in leadership team meetings for several weeks or months. However, participating in meetings is quite different from facilitating them effectively.

It can be valuable for leadership team members to take turns facilitating the leadership team Level 10 Meeting a few times before running their own departmental meetings, building their facilitation skills and confidence.

Developing Internal Facilitators: Not all leaders are naturally gifted facilitators, and that's perfectly okay. It's often effective to train and transition the facilitation role to someone else on the team who has strong facilitation skills, freeing the leader to participate fully rather than managing meeting logistics.

Whatever path you choose, remember that it takes practice to master facilitation skills and effective participation. Encourage team members to be open and honest when rating meetings and providing feedback, so everyone can continuously improve. Even experienced professionals need time to adapt to the Level 10 Meeting format. Some people will embrace it immediately, while others need several weeks to see the value and develop comfort with the structure.

☜ ***Mastery Tip:*** *Consider sharing the* How to Run World-Class Meetings *eBook from EOS Worldwide with meeting facilitators to help them learn Level 10 Meeting facilitation best practices. Download from the Rollout Resource Center at RolloutBook.com.*

DEPARTMENTAL SCORECARDS

When Scorecards are fully rolled out in departments, each team will have a Scorecard with five to fifteen numbers (hopefully, closer to five—less is more!) that make sense for this team to review and keep on track each week.

Reviewing the Scorecard in your departmental Level 10 Meeting should help you smoke out issues that can be solved by people in that department and create an environment of accountability where team members feel a sense of ownership for the activities they should engage in to drive results in the department.

Reviewing the departmental Scorecard during Level 10 Meetings serves several critical functions.

- **Early Problem Detection:** Numbers often reveal issues before they become visible through other means. A declining quality score might predict customer complaints before they arrive. Increasing cycle times might indicate capacity problems before delivery delays occur.

- **Shared Accountability:** When everyone sees the numbers together, it creates collective ownership of results rather than individual finger-pointing. The team naturally starts to help each other succeed rather than protecting individual territories.

- **Focus and Alignment:** Having clear, measurable targets helps everyone understand what "good performance" looks like and aligns daily efforts toward common goals.

- **Continuous Improvement:** Regularly reviewing trends over time helps teams identify patterns, test improvements, and celebrate progress systematically.

BUILDING YOUR DEPARTMENTAL SCORECARD

If you're not sure what numbers to track initially, you could start by "inheriting" relevant metrics from the leadership team's Scorecard, which typically already includes key numbers from each major department.

For example, if the leadership team Scorecard tracks:

- Weekly sales calls made
- Monthly recurring revenue
- Customer satisfaction scores
- Production units completed
- Cash flow and accounts receivable

Your Sales Department might inherit and expand on:

- Weekly sales calls made (by individual rep)
- Qualified leads generated
- Proposals submitted
- Close rate percentage
- Average deal size

Your Operations Department might track:

- Production units completed (by product line)
- Quality rejection rate
- On-time delivery percentage
- Safety incidents
- Inventory turns

Creating an effective departmental Scorecard means balancing insight with simplicity. Most successful teams discover that five to fifteen numbers provide the sweet spot—enough data to understand what's happening without overwhelming people with information they can't act on. Remember: less is more when it comes to meaningful measurement.

Your numbers should be available weekly to enable quick course corrections rather than waiting for month-end surprises. Each Measurable needs a clear owner who takes personal responsibility for trends and performance, along with a specific goal that makes "on track" versus "off track" reporting straightforward and honest.

The ultimate test for any number is whether it actually drives decisions or actions. If your team reviews a metric week after week without it sparking meaningful conversation or leading to concrete steps, question whether it deserves space on your Scorecard.

🖝 *Mastery Tip: For more detailed guidance on creating effective Scorecards, refer to Chapter 3 of the book* Data *by Mark O'Donnell, Mark Stanley, and Angela Kalemis.*

DEPARTMENTAL AND INDIVIDUAL ROCKS

When Rocks are fully rolled out throughout your organization, you'll have a powerful alignment system.

- **Leadership Team:** 3–7 company Rocks focused on strategic priorities
- **Each Department:** 3–7 departmental Rocks supporting company priorities
- **Each Individual:** 1–3 individual Rocks they're accountable for completing

This creates a cascade of focus from the leadership team down to individual accountability, ensuring that everyone's most important work is aligned with organizational priorities.

ROCK ETIQUETTE: THE RULES OF THE GAME

Before your departments start setting and managing Rocks, it's crucial to establish clear "Rock Etiquette"—the ground rules that make the Rock system work effectively. These aren't suggestions; they're essential disciplines that separate organizations that get real traction from those that just go through the motions. When you roll out these disciplines consistently from the start, your departments will adopt strong Rock habits rather than having to unlearn bad ones later.

Rock Due Dates: The foundation of Rock discipline starts with commitment to completion. Ideally, all Rocks in the company should be due on the day of the leadership team's Quarterly planning session, creating company-wide clarity and alignment. That said, "utopia" is not always possible, in which case you simply need to decide what your "rule" is. Are they due on the date of your departmental planning session? Are they due five days before the leadership team planning session to give everyone time to review deliverables? Decide on the rule, and then stick to it to create clarity and avoid confusion. And remember, if your Rock isn't 100 percent complete by the due date, it's not done—there's no partial credit!

Rock Completion Rate Expectations: In a company running on EOS, the expectation is 80 percent or better Rock completion quarter over quarter, meaning that 80 percent or more of all Rocks should be completed by the due date. Demonstrate this standard of performance consistently at the leadership team level, and reinforce it at the department and individual levels. If 80+ percent of your Rocks are being completed across the company, you'll gain traction.

Set Meaningful Rocks: Avoid the temptation to set Rocks that falsely inflate the Rock completion rate. Ideally, Rocks are meant to move the needle for the individual, department, or company, not to "check a box."

Weekly Reporting Must Be Honest and Lead to Action: When reporting on your Rock each week, you're either "on track" to complete it by quarter-end or you're "off track"—there's no middle ground. "On track" means you're confident you'll complete the Rock based on your current pace and remaining work. Don't sugarcoat it or report "on track" when you're really struggling. When a Rock goes off track, drop it down to the issues list immediately. Don't wait, don't hope it gets better, and don't suffer in silence. The sooner you surface obstacles, the sooner your team can help solve them.

No Mid-Quarter Changes: Once you set a Rock, you're committed for the full 90 days. The only acceptable reasons for changing a Rock mid-quarter are circumstances completely outside your control (like a key vendor going out of business) or situations where completing it would actually harm the business—and these should be *extremely rare exceptions* requiring team discussion. If this situation arises, you should discuss and decide as a team to cancel the Rock—people should not make unilateral decisions to abandon a Rock mid-quarter.

Following these best practices isn't about being rigid—it's about creating the discipline and accountability that makes Rocks a powerful tool for execution rather than just another planning exercise that people ignore.

SETTING DEPARTMENTAL ROCKS

In general, you'll get better buy-in and Rock completion if your team understands WHY a Rock is a priority and what issues it will solve. Some departmental teams are ready to participate in Rock setting right away, while others need a quarter or two of observing Rocks being managed and completed before they are ready to get involved.

If you don't think your team is ready to start participating in Rock setting, you may want to begin by "inheriting" company or individual Rocks that were set at the leadership team level and are relevant to specific departments.

For example, if your Sales and Marketing leader has a company or individual Rock to "Publish the Redesigned Website," you could list that Rock in the Sales and Marketing Level 10 Meeting, with the leader reporting "ON TRACK" or "OFF TRACK" each week and dropping down issues to discuss with the team.

When your team is ready, it's time to involve them in setting departmental Rocks during departmental Planning sessions.

QUARTERLY AND ANNUAL PLANNING IN DEPARTMENTS

Just as the leadership team needs regular planning sessions to stay aligned and focused, departments benefit from their own quarterly and annual planning pulse. These sessions ensure departmental priorities remain aligned with company goals while giving teams ownership of their specific challenges and opportunities.

QUARTERLY PLANNING IN DEPARTMENTS

Purpose:

- Review results from the previous quarter and reflect on lessons learned
- Realign on the vision for the company and department
- Set Rocks for the next quarter
- Solve key issues that require focused attention

Timing Considerations: Many companies hold their departmental Quarterlies *after* the leadership team Quarterly, allowing updated numbers, new Rocks, and vision refinements to be cascaded to departments during the V/TO review portion of their meetings.

This sequencing ensures that:

- Departmental priorities align with updated company priorities
- Leaders can share the latest strategic thinking and decisions
- Questions that arise at the departmental level can be addressed with current information
- Company momentum flows down through the organization systematically

That said, some companies choose to hold their departmental Quarterlies *before* the leadership team meets in order to surface issues that may need to be addressed at the leadership team level. Experiment to determine what works best for your organization.

ANNUAL PLANNING IN DEPARTMENTS

Purpose:

- Review results from the previous year and quarter; reflect on lessons learned
- Realign on the vision for the company, including updated 3-Year Picture, 1-Year Plan, and first quarter Rocks
- Set departmental Goals for the next year

- Set departmental Rocks for the next quarter
- Solve key issues that require focused attention

Key Difference from Quarterly: The Annual session includes setting departmental goals for the entire year, not just quarterly Rocks, and provides deeper reflection on longer-term trends and capabilities needed for success.

MEETING AGENDA OPTIONS

You have flexibility in how you structure these planning sessions.

Option 1: Extended Level 10 Meeting Format: Some teams conduct their planning within an extended Level 10 Meeting at the beginning of the quarter, taking extra time to review the V/TO and set goals/Rocks while maintaining the familiar meeting structure.

Option 2: Customize the Standard Planning Agenda: Other teams use the Quarterly/Annual Planning Agenda from Chapter 8 of Traction, adjusting the duration of each section to fit their allocated time.

Regardless of which format you choose, be sure to maintain focus and ensure that all essential elements are covered.

REAL WORLD EXAMPLE: PURPOSEFUL PLANNING

At CG Financial, a 70-person financial services firm, their departments started by "inheriting" Rocks from the leadership team for a quarter or two before beginning to set their own Rocks as a team. At first, they extended one of their Level 10 Meetings and set Rocks with very little discussion or debate, but this approach created a significant challenge: Without understanding the reasoning behind their Rocks, teams had little buy-in to actually achieve them.

Recognizing this disconnect, the leadership team redesigned their entire quarterly planning process. They implemented half-day quarterly planning meetings for each department, using a modified version of the standard Quarterly Pulsing Agenda compressed into a 4-hour time slot. These sessions were strategically scheduled after the leadership team Quarterly, allowing leaders to share prior quarter financial results and explain the rationale behind newly set Rocks.

For Annual Planning, they followed the same half-day planning cadence, reviewing results from the prior year, and setting two or three departmental goals that aligned with the company-level goals set for the upcoming year.

The transformation was remarkable. After just a couple of quarters with this new approach, the entire company developed a much deeper understanding of the company vision and how EOS tools were driving their progress. By investing time in explanation and collaborative planning, CG Financial turned Rock-setting from a top-down directive into a shared commitment that teams actually embraced. "You can feel and hear the alignment across the company now," reflects Visionary Tony Mazzali. "When people understand the why behind our decisions, they embrace change as being necessary rather than viewing it as frustrating."

☞ *Mastery Tip: For more detailed guidance on Quarterly and Annual planning agendas, see Chapter 8 of* Traction *by Gino Wickman.*

CREATING YOUR DEPARTMENTAL PLAN

So, how do you keep track of your Department's Goals and Rocks? On a Departmental Plan.

A Departmental Plan is simply the Traction page of the V/TO adapted to reflect departmental priorities and focus areas. It serves as each department's focused roadmap for tracking and achieving their contribution to company goals.

The Company V/TO remains unchanged and always travels with the Departmental Plan—you're just adding an additional Traction page (page 2 of the V/TO) for the department. Departments should not create their own Core Values, Core Focus, 10-Year Target, Marketing Strategy, or 3-Year Picture. Those belong to the company. Departments will have their own 1-Year Plan and Goals, Rocks, and Issues List on their Departmental Plan.

THE EOS PROCESS

THE VISION/TRACTION ORGANIZER™

ORGANIZATION NAME XYZ COMPANY - OPS DEPT.

———————————— TRACTION ————————————

1-YEAR PLAN	ROCKS		ISSUES LIST
FUTURE DATE: DECEMBER, 31 20XX	FUTURE DATE: MARCH, 31 20XX		1. EQUIPMENT UPGRADES
REVENUE: $15M	REVENUE: $4 M		
PROFIT: 12% NOP	PROFIT: 13% NOP		2. TRAINING GAPS
MEASURABLES: C-SAT 95%	MEASURABLES: C-SAT 90 %		3. SUPPLIER QUALITY CONCERNS
GOALS FOR THE YEAR:	ROCKS FOR THE QUARTER	WHO	4. _____
1. REDUCE PRODUCT DEFECTS 50%	1. IMPLEMENT QC PROC.	LEE	5. _____
2. OPS TRAINING DOC'D + FBA	2. AUDIT TRAINING DOCS	MIRIAM	6. _____
3. EQUIP PLAN DOC'D + FBA	3. EQUIP AUDIT DOC'D	JULIUS	7. _____
4. _____	4. _____		8. _____
5. _____	5. _____		9. _____
6. _____	6. _____		10. _____
7. _____	7. _____		

————————————————————————————— EOS

COMPONENTS OF A DEPARTMENTAL PLAN

- **Departmental 1-Year Goals:** 3–7 specific objectives that support company goals and align with your department's core function
- **Current Quarter Rocks:** 3–7 priorities for the next 90 days that move you toward your annual goals
- **Issues List:** Departmental challenges and long-term projects in the "parking lot" for future resolution

This simple tool creates powerful focus and alignment within each department while ensuring coordination with company-wide priorities and vision.

For example, if your company's goal is "Increase Customer Satisfaction to 95 percent," your Operations Departmental Plan might include:

- **1-Year Goal:** Reduce product defects by 50 percent
- **Q1 Rock:** Implement new quality control process
- **Issues List:** Equipment upgrade needs, training gaps, supplier quality concerns

VISION SHARED BY ALL: ENSURING TRUE UNDERSTANDING

Departmental Quarterly and Annual Planning meetings are a great opportunity to realign on the company's vision, ensuring your departmental team members understand where you're going and how their individual work contributes to the big picture.

Remember, you need to consistently share both the context (why these elements matter) and the content (what they actually say) of your V/TO for several quarters before your team can truly internalize them. During your first 2–4 depart-mental planning sessions and Level 10 Meetings, your team will still be getting familiar with EOS terms and the content of your V/TO.

Just as you spent time at the leadership level repeatedly reviewing and discussing each element of your vision until it became second nature, your departmental teams need that same repetition and reinforcement. While they may nod and say they understand after the first few exposures, it's important to check whether they truly grasp how these concepts apply to their daily work.

After you've consistently shared both the context and content for a couple of quarters, you can begin checking for genuine understanding. This isn't about testing people; it's about ensuring everyone has the clarity they need to make good decisions and contribute effectively to your vision. **Help them connect the dots between the vision and reality, and they'll help you make your vision a reality.**

SAMPLE UNDERSTANDING CHECK QUESTIONS

Core Values

- "Who can tell me why we have core values?"
- "What are our core values, and can you explain what each one means in your daily work?"
- "Can you give me an example of how you lived our core value [insert specific value] this quarter?"

Core Focus

- "Why do we have a Core Focus, and how does it help us make decisions?"

- "Are all of our current people, systems, and processes aligned to support our Core Focus?"
- "Can you think of a situation this quarter where we used our Core Focus to make a decision?"

10-Year Target

- "What is our 10-Year Target, and why is it important to achieve?"
- "How does your department contribute to reaching our 10-Year Target?"
- "What excites you most about what we're building toward?"

Marketing Strategy

- "What does our Marketing Strategy do for us as a company?"
- "Who is our ideal customer, and why do they choose us?"
- "How do you see our 3 Uniques showing up in your daily work?"

Process and Operations

- "Who can walk us through our Proven Process and explain each step?"
- "How does our Guarantee/Promise affect how you approach your work?"
- "What processes in your department could be improved to better serve our customers?"

Future Vision

- "What does our 3-Year Picture mean for our department specifically?"
- "How do this year's goals connect to our longer-term vision?"
- "What skills or capabilities will we need to develop to achieve our vision?"

These questions reveal whether your team truly understands the vision or if they're just nodding along politely. Real understanding shows up in their ability to explain concepts in their own words and connect them to their specific work and responsibilities.

Remember CG Financial's approach to purposeful quarterly and annual planning? A major benefit to implementing these sessions in Departments was the additional depth in understanding gained by team members during the V/TO review. When a financial advisor was asked, "How does our Core Focus, 'Helping People Achieve Lifelong Goals,' help us make decisions?" she initially gave a textbook answer about their focus statement. When pressed with "Can you give me a specific example from last quarter?" she described how they had changed how client review meetings were conducted, spending more time learning about their hopes and dreams rather than focusing solely on portfolio performance. That's when you know someone truly gets it—they can connect abstract concepts to real decisions they've made.

THE RIPPLE EFFECT

As you roll out EOS tools systematically to your departments, you'll begin to see the ripple effect that makes EOS so powerful for organizational transformation.

- **Improved Issue Resolution:** Problems that used to bubble up to the leadership team get solved efficiently at the departmental level by the people closest to the work who understand the context and have the authority to implement solutions.

- **Enhanced Communication:** Regular Level 10 Meetings create predictable communication cadences that prevent small issues from becoming big problems and ensure everyone stays aligned on priorities and progress.

- **Increased Accountability:** Weekly Rock reporting and Scorecard reviews create healthy peer pressure and personal ownership, driving higher performance and follow-through.

- **Better Decision-Making:** When everyone understands the vision and has clear priorities, they make better decisions independently, reducing bottlenecks and increasing organizational agility.

- **Higher Engagement:** People feel more connected to the company's success when they understand how their work contributes to meaningful goals and can clearly see their progress.

- **Reduced Leadership Burden:** As departments become more self-managing and effective, leaders can focus on strategic opportunities rather than operational firefighting.

Remember that patience and flexibility are key when rolling out EOS tools at the departmental level. Some teams will embrace these changes more readily than others, while some may need more time and support to be successful. Check in periodically, celebrate success when you see it, and encourage continuous improvement wherever possible.

✂ *Rollout Tool:* *Running into challenges? The Rollout Troubleshooting Guide in Appendix D addresses the 10 most common Rollout issues with specific symptoms, root causes, and solutions.*

CHAPTER 7 SUMMARY

Moving from company-wide awareness to departmental implementation requires a systematic Rollout of Level 10 Meetings, Scorecards, and Rocks within each team, creating focus and accountability at the operational level.

Key elements of effective departmental Rollout include:

- **Departmental Level 10 Meetings** with proper facilitation, appropriate frequency, and meaningful participation from people who can drive results.

- **Departmental Scorecards** with 5–15 weekly Measurables that enable early problem detection and create shared ownership.

- **Departmental and Individual Rocks** that cascade from company priorities to individual accountability.

- **Quarterly and Annual Planning** that aligns departmental goals with company vision, while giving teams ownership of their challenges.

- **Understanding Checks** to ensure team members truly grasp how EOS concepts apply to their daily work.

The transformation creates a ripple effect: issues are solved by the people closest to the work, communication becomes more predictable, accountability increases through ownership, and the leadership burden decreases as departments become self-managing.

Different approaches work for different organizations— some roll out one tool at a time across all departments, others introduce multiple tools simultaneously, and some focus on one department at a time. What's most important is choosing an approach that fits your organization's capacity for change while maintaining the integrity of each EOS tool's structure and methodology.

By having departmental EOS practices take root through-out your organization, you've created the structural foundation for lasting change. Yet structure alone isn't enough to transform culture. The most powerful impact of Rollout happens when your vision stops being something you talk about in meetings and becomes part of how your organization operates every single day. This means integrating the vision into hiring decisions, daily operations, customer interactions, and strategic choices. It's time to move from implementing tools to embodying the vision in everything you do.

What's Next: In Chapter 8, we'll explore how to bring your vision to life by integrating key elements of the V/TO in the day-to-day operations of the business.

REFLECTION QUESTIONS

1. **Departmental structure and readiness**: How should we define "departments" for Rollout purposes based on

who works together regularly? Which teams are ready to start Level 10 Meetings now, and which need more preparation?

2. **Scorecards and accountability**: What numbers from our leadership Scorecard could form the foundation of departmental Scorecards? How will we ensure each department has meaningful metrics they can actually influence?

3. **Rollout approach**: Should we roll out one tool at a time across all departments, implement all tools in one department first, or take a hybrid approach? What factors in our organization should influence this decision?

4. **True understanding**: How will we check whether our team truly understands the vision and EOS concepts beyond just nodding along? What will we do when we discover gaps in understanding?

8

BRINGING YOUR VISION TO LIFE

Dreams do not come true just because you dream them. It's hard work that makes things happen. It's hard work that creates change.

—Shonda Rhimes

As your Integration deepens throughout departments, this chapter focuses on the most transformative aspect: bringing your vision to life in everything you do.

This chapter isn't about developing your V/TO—you've already done that important work. It's about transforming your vision from words on paper into the living, breathing DNA of how your organization operates every day.

Creating and sharing your vision is only the beginning. The real work lies in weaving these elements into the daily fabric of how your organization makes decisions, serves customers, and solves problems.

Your V/TO consists of two interconnected pages: the Vision page defines where you're going, and the Traction page maps out how you're going to get there. What separates successful organizations from those that struggle is that they treat their V/TO as a daily decision-making tool rather than just a document they review quarterly.

True transformation happens when every element of your V/TO becomes integrated into how you hire team members, evaluate opportunities, and make decisions on a daily basis. When your vision becomes this embedded in your operations, it creates a powerful competitive advantage that's difficult for others to replicate.

It's time to move beyond talking about your vision and start proving, through your actions, that every decision moves you closer to achieving it.

CREATING AN INTENTIONAL CULTURE

To build a truly great culture, you must hire, fire, review, reward, and recognize using your Core Values. Gino Wickman's challenge to every leadership team is simple but brutal: You must "reek" of your organization's Core Values.

If you're not authentically living your Core Values every day, nobody else will either. And nothing destroys credibility faster than a leader who delivers an inspiring Core Values Speech at the company meeting and then completely contradicts those values in the hallway five minutes later.

Think about it this way: If your Core Values truly define who you are, then every person joining your team should embody them, every performance conversation should reference them, and every bit of recognition should celebrate them. When this happens consistently (and yes, it takes discipline), your Core Values become the living, breathing foundation of your culture rather than the forgotten words buried in the employee handbook.

ALIGNING YOUR HR SYSTEMS WITH EOS

Before implementing Core Values-based practices, many organizations find it helpful to review how their existing HR policies and performance management systems can work alongside EOS tools. If you're an HR professional reading this, your expertise in people systems, training, and change management is valuable throughout this process. The opportunity is figuring out how your knowledge can work with EOS principles rather than compete with them.

Many organizations discover that EOS naturally complements their people practices. The Accountability Chart can clarify role definitions, Rocks can drive performance conversations, Measurables can create objective feedback, and Core Values can guide cultural decisions. The question becomes: How can your existing systems work together with these tools to create even better outcomes?

Some organizations choose to simplify certain practices—perhaps replacing lengthy review processes with Quarterly Conversations, or aligning job descriptions with Accountability Chart language. Others find ways to enhance their current systems using EOS data and insights. There's no single "right" approach, and what works will depend on your industry, location, regulatory requirements, and organizational culture.

For HR leaders, this integration often creates opportunities to focus more on strategic people development and less on administrative processes. Your role in helping people succeed becomes even more important as EOS tools provide clearer frameworks for performance and development conversations.

The goal is ensuring that your people practices and EOS principles reinforce each other rather than creating competing expectations. Consider what adjustments, if any, would help your team experience greater clarity and alignment in how performance, development, and cultural fit are understood and supported.

HIRING FOR CULTURAL FIT

Your hiring process represents your first and most important opportunity to bring Core Values to life operationally. Every new hire either strengthens or dilutes your culture, so getting this right is critical.

ATTRACTING THE RIGHT PEOPLE

Start by examining how you attract potential employees to your organization. Your Core Values should be prominently featured in every job posting, on your careers page, and in recruitment material—not tucked away at the bottom like legal fine print that nobody reads.

Create compelling narratives about your culture that naturally weave your Core Values into the story of what it's really like to work at your organization. For example, if one of your Core Values is "continuous learning," don't just list that phrase. Instead, describe how your team members are constantly growing through new challenges, how mistakes become learning opportunities rather than sources of blame, and how professional development is prioritized and supported.

Feature these authentic culture descriptions everywhere potential candidates might discover you: on your careers page, team page, social media profiles, employee testimonials, and recruitment materials. The goal is attracting people who read these descriptions and think, "Finally, a place where I might actually fit in and thrive."

SCREENING FOR CORE VALUES

Once you've attracted candidates who are genuinely drawn to your culture, your interview process needs to check whether they truly align with your Core Values. This means developing specific, behavior-based questions designed to reveal how candidates naturally think and behave when your core values come into play.

Everyone involved in the interview process needs to consistently ask these Core Value-based questions. It can't just be the hiring manager's responsibility—every interviewer should understand how to identify whether candidates share your values and can provide evidence of living them in previous situations.

This creates consistency across all interviews and ensures that cultural alignment gets the same rigorous attention as technical skills and experience.

Mastery Tip: For more detailed guidance on hiring and getting the Right People in the Right Seats, see Chapter 8 of People *by Mark O'Donnell, Kelly Knight, and CJ Dubé.*

ONBOARDING AND TRAINING

Your work doesn't end when someone accepts your offer. The onboarding process represents make-or-break time—the period where new employees either fully embrace your Core Values and feel excited about the culture they've joined, or start viewing them as corporate fluff that doesn't match reality.

Make your Core Values absolutely central to your training program, not a brief side note during orientation. Repeat them frequently, but more importantly, connect the dots between daily work situations and how they relate to your values in practical application.

New hires should complete their first few weeks with a crystal-clear understanding not just of what your Core Values are, but also of how they show up in real work situations, decision-making processes, and interpersonal interactions. When they see these connections early and often, they're much more likely to internalize the values as part of their own approach to work and relationships.

REAL-WORLD EXAMPLE: SKIDMORE SALES AND DISTRIBUTING CO.

After getting feedback from new employees at their 30-day check-ins, Skidmore discovered they had a communication problem. HR leader Dennis Purcell heard the same complaint repeatedly: "I start on Monday, and Tuesday I find out I'm in something called a Level 10 Meeting, and they're talking about Rocks and Issues—and I have no idea what they're talking about."

The leadership team realized they were throwing new hires into the deep end of EOS without teaching them how to swim. "We assumed people would pick up the terminology through osmosis," Dennis reflected. "Instead, we were creating confusion and anxiety during their most important first weeks."

Now at Skidmore, new employees go through a comprehensive onboarding process that includes EOS orientation on their first day. They receive a copy of "What the Heck is EOS?" along with a clear overview of EOS terminology and how it applies to their daily work. The training also includes in-person sessions on Core Values and the V/TO, connecting these concepts to their specific role and responsibilities.

The transformation has been dramatic. New employees now participate confidently in their first Level 10 Meetings instead of sitting silently, confused by the language around them. "It's really important to get people speaking the same language from the beginning," Dennis explains. "When everyone understands the vocabulary, they can focus on contributing to the vision instead of just trying to decode what we're talking about."

BUILDING RELATIONSHIPS THAT REINFORCE CULTURE

Traditional performance reviews often fail to create meaningful change or alignment. Quarterly Conversations are informal but structured 90-day check-ins between managers and direct reports, focused on what's working and what's not across three key areas: how well someone is living your Core Values, whether they're clear on their role and executing their responsibilities, and whether they're hitting their quarterly Rocks and Measurables. Both the manager and the employee prepare by thinking through the same areas, creating real dialogue rather than a one-sided evaluation.

ADDRESSING CULTURAL MISALIGNMENT

Let's be honest: No hiring process is perfect, and even people who initially seem aligned with your Core Values might struggle to live them consistently. This is where many organizations fail—they either ignore the problem and let their culture slowly erode, or they approach correction in ways that create fear rather than growth.

When someone's behavior doesn't align with your Core Values, the **3-Strike Rule** provides a systematic approach that's both firm and fair. It involves a direct conversation about the misalignment, a follow-up to assess improvement, and finally helping them find a better cultural fit if they can't consistently live your values. This approach combines clear expectations with genuine opportunities for improvement, so people know exactly where they stand while your team sees you're serious about protecting the culture you've committed to building together.

RECOGNITION THAT REINFORCES VALUES

Here's what we've learned: the behaviors you recognize and reward are the behaviors you'll see more of. This makes recognition one of your most powerful tools for embedding Core Values throughout your organization.

There are countless ways to weave Core Value recognition into your regular communication. For example, you could use the headlines portion of Level 10 Meetings to highlight examples of people living your values. Or you could implement Core Value shout-outs during team huddles or quarterly State of the Company meetings. When people hear specific examples of colleagues embodying your values, it reinforces what those values actually look like in action.

Some organizations create formal Core Values awards where employees nominate peers. This peer recognition carries special weight because it comes from people who actually work closely with the nominees and can speak to their day-to-day behavior. Don't overlook digital recognition through tools like Slack, Microsoft Teams, or whatever communication platform your team uses—these ongoing, informal shout-outs create a steady cadence of Core Value awareness.

Public recognition creates positive peer pressure—people naturally want to be recognized and celebrated by their colleagues, so highlighting Core Value behaviors makes those behaviors more attractive to everyone.

Mastery Tip: For more detailed guidance on reviewing, rewarding, and recognizing, see How to Be a Great Boss *by Gino Wickman and René Boer. You'll also learn more about these disciplines when you learn LMA (Leadership, Management, and Accountability) if you're working with a Professional EOS Implementer.*

Rollout Planning Tip: Review your current hiring, review, and recognition processes to identify the specific changes you'll need to authentically integrate core values.

STAYING FOCUSED

Your biggest enemy isn't your competition; it's your own scattered energy. Every entrepreneurial leader knows what it feels like to have a million great ideas and not enough focus to execute any of them exceptionally well. Use your V/TO as a tool to help you stay focused on doing the things that will help you get closer to your vision.

Your **Core Focus** defines your organization's sweet spot—the intersection of your purpose, what you're passionate about, and your niche, what you can be best in the world at. When properly implemented, it becomes the filter for every opportunity that comes your way. Use it to evaluate new opportunities, partnerships, and initiatives. If something doesn't align with your purpose, leverage your unique strengths, or contribute to your economic engine, it's probably a distraction regardless of how attractive it might seem in isolation.

REAL-WORLD EXAMPLE: USING CORE FOCUS AS A STRATEGIC FILTER

When a high-end custom cake bakery known for creating stunning cakes decided to add a café to its existing successful operations, the leadership team thought, "How hard could it be?" The owners soon found themselves working 80 to 100 hours per week just to ensure proper staffing. The added operational complexity was draining their energy and focus—and to top it off, they were losing profitability. That's when they decided to implement EOS.

After clarifying their Core Focus—Passion: To create "wow" experiences; Niche: Amazing Desserts and Food—they had the framework to evaluate whether the café really fit. For several quarters, their EOS Implementer kept asking: "Is the café a distraction? It feels like it's draining your energy. What would it look like if you simplified?"

The breakthrough came during a Quarterly after looking hard at the numbers—and at the number of issues on their Issues List related to the café. They finally had the courage to shut down café operations. They updated their Niche to read simply: "Amazing Desserts." This clarification became their strategic filter for evaluating every service, partnership, and business opportunity moving forward.

The results were immediate and measurable. The company returned to profitability within one quarter. Processes were simplified. Their Issues List was no longer overwhelming. The culture improved significantly. Most importantly, they could focus all their energy on what they were truly passionate about and exceptional at—creating amazing desserts that deliver "wow" experiences.

One customer captured the significance of their decision: "That was a brave decision to let go of the café. Many business owners would rather go out of business than look foolish in the community. Congratulations on making the right decision for your company."

Your **3-Year Picture** is a vivid description of your future reality that should influence how you operate today. Use it to guide strategic decisions about hiring, systems, and capabilities so that every major decision moves you closer to that future state. When team members understand where you're heading, they can make better choices about priorities and resource allocation. This is also a great opportunity to connect the dots and help your team see what's in it for them while also acknowledging the issues you are working to solve in the coming years.

Your **1-Year Goals** represent the specific, measurable outcomes that will move you significantly closer to your 3-Year Picture. These aren't just targets—they're commitments that require focused execution and regular attention. Goals are the three to seven (not thirty-seven) most important things you need to get done in the next twelve months. These goals should advance the company and help you move closer to achieving your 3-Year Picture.

Your **Rocks** are your most important priorities for the next 90 days, representing the specific projects and outcomes that will move you closer to your annual goals and long-term vision. As you set Rocks each quarter, look back at your 1-Year Plan to ensure you are making progress toward completing your goals by the end of the year. The key to successful Rock execution is limiting yourself to what actually matters most. Most teams try to accomplish too much and end up achieving too little. Choose fewer Rocks and execute them exceptionally rather than spreading your energy across too many initiatives.

Finally, don't forget to use the **Issues List** to compartmentalize your issues. While the Issues List in your Level 10 Meeting should be used for issues that need to be addressed in the current quarter, the Issues List on your V/TO should be reserved for long-term issues you are strategically choosing not to solve in the next 90 Days. Having the discipline to distinguish between short-term and long-term issues helps you stay focused.

As you make decisions throughout the year, be sure to connect the dots for your team - remind them why you are saying yes or no to spending time on something and tie your decision back to your vision whenever possible. Remember: when everything is important, nothing is important. It's all about staying focused.

MAKING A BIG IMPACT

Your 10-Year Target isn't just an aspirational goal; it's the North Star that should influence every major decision you make today. When properly implemented, it creates urgency, focuses resources, and inspires your team to think bigger than they might otherwise.

As Dan Sullivan, Founder and President of The Strategic Coach®, says, "The only way to make your present better is by making your future bigger." Every major decision should be evaluated against whether it moves you closer to or further from your 10-Year Target. This includes decisions about markets to enter, products to develop, people to hire, and systems to implement. Your target should also influence how you allocate resources, with investments that accelerate progress toward your target deserving priority over those that don't, even if the alternatives seem attractive in isolation.

Share your 10-Year Target widely throughout your organization so that when people understand the bigger impact you're working toward, their daily work takes on greater meaning and purpose. Use it to attract top talent who want to be part of something significant—great people are drawn to organizations with ambitious visions and clear paths for achieving them.

While your 10-Year Target might seem far away, you should be able to regularly measure progress toward it by identifying the key metrics that indicate you're on track and consistently reviewing them. Celebrate milestones along the way to maintain momentum and reinforce that you're making real progress toward your ultimate vision.

REAL WORLD EXAMPLE: SHOWING VISIBLE PROGRESS

Meadowlark Design + Build, a 40-person residential construction company in Ann Arbor, Michigan, set a 10-Year Target to "Improve 1,000 spaces by 2030." Integrator Melissa Kennedy knew that her team would be energized by a visible reminder of their progress toward the target, so she had a metal sign created with 1,000 empty circles cut into it and mounted it in the hallway of the office. As each client project is completed, the team gathers to fill a circle with a metal disc bearing the Meadowlark logo. "Our team tells me that the sign helps remind them that they are part of something bigger than themselves, and it's also a great conversation starter when clients and prospective employees visit the office."

ATTRACTING IDEAL CUSTOMERS

Your Target Market definition should drive every marketing and sales decision you make. It's not enough to know who your ideal customers are—you must focus all your customer-facing activities on attracting and serving them exceptionally well.

```
┌─────────────────┐
│     TARGET      │
│     MARKET      │
│  ─────────────  │
│   "THE LIST"    │
│    • DEMO       │
│    • GEO        │
│    • PSYCH      │
└─────────────────┘
```

FOCUSING YOUR MARKETING

Use your Target Market to develop messaging and content that speaks directly to your ideal customers' challenges and aspirations. Every piece of marketing should be created with this specific audience in mind, not some vague "everyone who has money and might buy from us" approach.

Your marketing team should understand the demographic, geographic, and psychographic characteristics of your target market so they can choose the right channels, craft the right messages, and create the right content to attract these specific people to your organization.

When your marketing is truly focused on your target market, you'll attract more qualified leads who are genuinely interested in what you offer and willing to pay for the value you provide.

QUALIFYING SALES PROSPECTS

Your sales team should use your Target Market definition to identify and qualify prospects. They should be able to quickly determine whether a potential customer fits your ideal profile and prioritize their time accordingly.

Train your salespeople to ask the right questions to assess target-market fit early in the sales process. This prevents wasted time pursuing prospects who aren't likely to become great customers, regardless of their ability to pay.

When both marketing and sales operate from the same clear picture of your ideal customer, your entire go-to-market approach becomes more focused and effective at attracting and converting the right people.

DIFFERENTIATING YOURSELF FROM THE COMPETITION

Your 3 Uniques, Proven Process, and Guarantee work together to create clear differentiation from your competitors. The key is that they only create competitive advantage when they're consistently communicated and experienced by customers.

MAKING YOUR 3 UNIQUES TANGIBLE

Your 3 Uniques are the heart of your differentiation, but they only work if people actually understand and experience them. This requires more than just listing them in a document—you need to weave them into everything you do.

In Marketing: Create dedicated content that showcases your uniqueness in action. Develop case studies, testimonials, and demonstrations that prove you deliver on what makes you different. Don't just claim your Uniques; provide evidence of them.

In Sales: Ensure every salesperson can articulate your 3 Uniques through compelling stories and examples. They should connect each unique to specific customer benefits and be able to clearly explain how you're different from competitors. Consider crafting an "elevator pitch" for your sales team to deliver consistently, highlighting what sets you apart.

In Operations: This is where differentiation is won or lost. Your delivery team must consistently deliver on the promises your Uniques represent. If marketing and sales promise something your delivery team can't consistently deliver, you'll create customer disappointment rather than loyalty.

REAL-WORLD EXAMPLE: MAKING YOUR 3 UNIQUES COME ALIVE

When Güd Marketing, a social impact marketing agency in Lansing, Michigan, clarified their 3 Uniques—Trusted Partner, Category Experts, and Problem Solvers—Integrator Julie Kruger and Visionary Deb Horak knew that simply documenting them wasn't enough. They needed everyone in the organization to truly understand them, communicate them in a compelling way, and, most importantly, live them consistently.

"We use our 3 Uniques as a selling point to attract our target market, represent us authentically, and differentiate us from the competition," Julie explains. "We also educate our internal account teams to use the 3 Uniques

"We use our 3 Uniques as a selling point to attract our target market, represent us authentically, and differentiate us from the competition," Julie explains. "We also educate our internal account teams to use the 3 Uniques to continue educating clients while also demonstrating them in every interaction. For example, if we're saying we are problem solvers, we need to align our behavior with that or else our clients will be disappointed."

To ensure their 3 Uniques became embedded in daily operations rather than just marketing copy, Güd set a 1-Year company goal: "The 3 Uniques are Clear and Adopted Across the Agency." Deb then took on Rocks to develop comprehensive training—first to educate the entire team, then to help the Sales and Account teams build confidence in communicating and demonstrating their differentiators in compelling ways.

The shift was immediate and impactful. Instead of just reciting content, team members now really understand what makes Güd different. They work together to communicate their 3 Uniques naturally—in client presentations, internal discussions, and daily decision-making. The result is authentic differentiation that clients experience consistently, not just promises in a proposal.

DEMONSTRATING YOUR PROVEN PROCESS

Your Proven Process is a visual representation of the repeatable steps your team follows to ensure quality outcomes for every customer. Think of it as your recipe for success. Use your Proven Process throughout the customer journey to set, manage, and deliver on expectations, and differentiate yourself from competitors who can't articulate their methodology.

PROVEN PROCESS

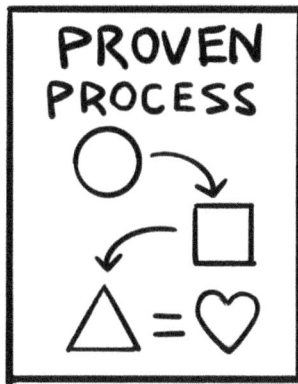

In Marketing: Use your Proven Process in content and campaigns to demonstrate your methodology and build confidence in your approach. Show prospects exactly how you'll deliver value, not just what you'll deliver.

In Sales: Present your Proven Process during sales conversations to set clear expectations about what working with you will be like. This differentiates you from competitors who can't articulate how they do what they do and helps prospects visualize the experience of being your customer.

In Operations: Once customers are on board, use your Proven Process to manage their expectations and show them where they are in the journey. Ensure your team understands how to deliver on what sales promised, with operational processes aligned to consistently meet those expectations.

When your Proven Process becomes embedded across marketing, sales, and operations, it transforms from a pretty picture to a competitive advantage customers can feel.

REAL-WORLD EXAMPLE: ALIGNING THE ENTIRE ORGANIZATION AROUND CLIENT EXPERIENCE

When HOH Water Technology finally tackled their Proven Process after it sat on their issues list for years, the transformation went far beyond marketing and sales. The breakthrough came when Integrator Reid Hutchison and the leadership team attended an EOS Conference break-out session on Marketing Strategy, where they realized that graphically representing their client experience could solve multiple operational challenges simultaneously.

HOH's leadership had previously viewed their Proven Process as purely a marketing exercise. The paradigm shift occurred when they mapped out their six-phase client journey: Discover, Develop, Commit, Deliver, Review, and Plan. What emerged wasn't just a sales tool—it was a comprehensive operational framework that aligned their entire organization.

The impact rippled through every department. Marketing could create targeted content for each phase, addressing specific client concerns and demonstrating expertise at every touchpoint. Their sales team gained clarity on exactly what they were selling at each phase, moving beyond generic promises to specific, repeatable outcomes. The Field Service Team, previously unclear about their role in the broader client experience, now understood how their work connected to client satisfaction and retention.

Most significantly, the visual representation of their process became a client communication tool. Prospects could see exactly what working with HOH would look like, reducing uncertainty and building confidence in their methodology. Existing clients gained reassurance about HOH's commitment to them throughout the entire relationship, not just during the initial sale.

The leadership team now recognizes their Proven Process as more than a marketing asset—it's an operational alignment tool that ensures everyone understands what the client experience should look like. By making their methodology visible and repeatable, HOH transformed from a company that delivered good results inconsistently to one that systematically delivers exceptional client experiences through every phase of their relationship.

BUILDING CONFIDENCE WITH YOUR GUARANTEE

Your Guarantee gives customers confidence that choosing you is a safe decision. It demonstrates your commitment to delivering on your promises and shows that you stand behind your work.

In Marketing: Feature your guarantee prominently to demonstrate your confidence in your ability to deliver exceptional results. Use it to reduce the perceived risk of choosing you over competitors.

In Sales: Use your guarantee to overcome objections and close deals by showing prospects you stand behind your work. Connect it to your 3 Uniques and Proven Process to show why you can make such a commitment.

In Operations: Make sure your team knows how to honor your guarantee when customers invoke it. Train them on the process for quickly addressing customer concerns and for standing behind your commitments without creating friction or making customers jump through hoops.

Your guarantee should align with your 3 Uniques and be supported by your Proven Process. When all these elements work together, your guarantee becomes a natural extension of the value you provide rather than a risky commitment you're not sure you can keep.

REAL-WORLD EXAMPLE: A GUARANTEE THAT CREATES CONFIDENCE

LeadingIT demonstrates the power of a customer-centric guarantee with their bold promise: "Onboarding and Support You'll Love—or Your Money Back."

What makes this guarantee exceptional is the direct accountability it creates. LeadingIT commits to delivering exactly what they promised within the first 100 days of service, to the client's satisfaction. If clients aren't satisfied with their onboarding or support, LeadingIT will refund three months of payments—no questions asked.

"We don't want clients to just like our service, we want them to love it," explains Integrator Laura Piekos. "Our guarantee puts our money where our mouth is. Accountability is one of our core values, and this promise holds us to it. If we don't deliver exactly what we promised in those first 100 days, we'll make it right and refund you, simple as that."

The guarantee has become more than just a risk-reduction tool—it's a competitive differentiator that demonstrates LeadingIT's confidence in their service quality and commitment to delivering on their promises. "In an industry with zero guarantees, we're the outliers—risking our revenues to prove we're all-in," declares Visionary Stephen Taylor. "No empty promises or platitudes, clients get great results or they don't pay. We are betting our success on their satisfaction."

The result is a guarantee that doesn't just close sales—it creates a culture of accountability throughout the organization and drives genuine focus on delivering the onboarding and support experience that clients will genuinely love.

CREATING A GREAT CUSTOMER EXPERIENCE

The same elements that differentiate you from competitors—your 3 Uniques, Proven Process, and Guarantee—also drive exceptional customer experiences when they're consistently delivered throughout the customer journey. It's a powerful equation:

DELIVERING ON YOUR 3 UNIQUES

Your operations team must consistently deliver on the promises your 3 Uniques represent. This is where customer satisfaction is won or lost. Every customer interaction should reinforce what makes you different and special.

Train your entire team to understand your 3 Uniques and how their role contributes to delivering them. When everyone understands how they contribute to your differentiation, they're more likely to make decisions that enhance rather than undermine the customer experience.

FOLLOWING YOUR PROVEN PROCESS

Use your Proven Process consistently to ensure every customer receives the same high-quality experience. This creates predictability and reliability that customers value and competitors struggle to match.

Your account managers should use your Proven Process to manage expectations, showing customers where they are in the journey and what comes next. This transparency builds trust and reduces anxiety about the unknown.

When you consistently follow your Proven Process, it becomes a powerful tool for maintaining the quality and consistency that your 3 Uniques promise.

STANDING BEHIND YOUR GUARANTEE

Ensure your delivery capabilities support your Guarantee. If you can't confidently deliver on your promise, strengthen your operations rather than weakening your Guarantee.

When customers know you stand behind your work, they're more likely to trust you with important projects and recommend you to others. Your Guarantee becomes a competitive advantage that builds long-term relationships rather than just closing individual sales.

BRINGING IT ALL TOGETHER

When all these elements work together consistently, they create a powerful reinforcement cycle throughout your organization. Your culture attracts the right people who use your V/TO as a decision-making tool to stay focused on what matters most while working toward a shared long-term vision of success. Your marketing attracts ideal customers who appreciate your unique value and enjoy working with you. Your differentiated approach creates exceptional experiences that turn customers into advocates.

This consistency creates something genuinely powerful: an organization where your vision is truly brought to life. It isn't just words on a poster or website, but the actual operating principles that guide how people think, make decisions, and interact with each other and your customers every single day.

Mastery Tip: The Rollout Troubleshooting Guide in Appendix D provides specific solutions and strategies for handling common Rollout challenges.

CHAPTER 8 SUMMARY

The key insight is that scattered energy, not competition, is your biggest enemy. Your V/TO only creates competitive advantage when it moves from words on a page to being integrated into daily operations. When your vision becomes the operational framework for daily decisions, it creates focus that's incredibly difficult for competitors to replicate:

- **Creating an intentional culture** by using your Core Values as the foundation for hiring, performance reviews, and recognition.

- **Staying focused** by treating your Core Focus, 3-Year Picture, 1-Year Plan and Goals, and Rocks as an integrated decision-making filter.

- **Making a big impact** by using your 10-Year Target as the North Star for measuring progress and providing team inspiration.

- **Attracting ideal customers** by operationalizing your Target Market across all marketing and sales activities.

- **Differentiating yourself from competition** by consistently delivering on your 3 Uniques, using your Proven Process and Guarantee.

- **Creating a great customer experience** by ensuring the same elements that differentiate you also drive exceptional service delivery.

Remember that "vision without traction is hallucination." When all elements work together consistently, they create a reinforcement cycle where culture attracts the right people, focus drives results, and vision guides every decision.

What's Next: In Chapter 9, we'll explore how EOS helps you create an environment of accountability that will help you gain traction to achieve your vision.

REFLECTION QUESTIONS

1. **Creating an Intentional Culture**: How consistently do we use our Core Values when we hire, fire, review, reward, and recognize? What specific changes would make them more central to how we operate?

2. **Staying Focused**: What opportunities or initiatives are we currently pursuing that don't align with our Core Focus? What would happen if we stopped them to focus on what matters most?

3. **Making a Big Impact**: Is this goal big and energizing for everyone in the company? Are we making steady progress toward our 10-Year Target?

4. **Attracting Ideal Customers**: What percentage of our marketing efforts specifically target our ideal customer profile versus trying to appeal to everyone? How well can our sales team identify prospects who truly fit?

5. **Differentiating Yourself from the Competition**: Can every customer-facing team member clearly explain our 3 Uniques and provide evidence of how we deliver them consistently?

6. **Creating a Great Customer Experience**: Are we using our Proven Process to set, manage, and deliver on expectations to create an exceptional customer experience? Is our guarantee helping us close business and give our customers peace of mind?

9

CREATING AN ENVIRONMENT OF ACCOUNTABILITY

A leader is one who knows the way,
goes the way, and shows the way.

—Rosabeth Moss Kanter

As the vision becomes integrated into daily operations and your departmental EOS practices take root, you've created something powerful: the structural foundation for genuine accountability. Your Accountability Chart eliminates confusion about roles, your Level 10 Meetings create transparent reporting, and your Rocks and Scorecards drive focused execution.

Every step you've taken—from clarifying expectations through your Accountability Chart to creating weekly reporting disciplines in your Level 10 Meetings—has been systematically building an environment where accountable people thrive and those who resist accountability become visible.

The five EOS Foundational Tools you've been rolling out don't just create clarity and focus—they create natural accountability. When people understand their role, report their numbers weekly, and commit to quarterly Rocks in front of their colleagues, accountability stops feeling forced and becomes the natural way of operating.

Now that your Foundational Tools are working well throughout your organization, two additional tools will complete your accountability foundation and address the remaining gaps in organizational clarity: the 3-Step Process Documenter and ensuring everyone has a number they're accountable for.

As Gino Wickman says in Chapter 10 of *Traction*, "Implementing [the EOS Foundational Tools] into your entire company produces 80 percent of the results."[5] When you have the five EOS Foundational Tools rolled out, there are two other tools and disciplines to introduce to your team: 3-Step Process Documenter and Measureables (everyone has a number).

1. V/TO
2. The Accountability Chart
3. Rocks
4. The Meeting Pulse
5. Scorecard
6. 3-Step Process Documenter
7. Measureables (everyone has a number)

These two additional tools, combined with leadership development through LMA (Leadership, Management, and Accountability), will help you achieve the final 20 percent by ensuring everyone knows exactly what's expected of them and how their individual contributions connect to organizational success.

Before we explore these additional tools and disciplines, let's pause and recognize what you've already accomplished with the Foundational Tools.

THE POWER OF CLEAR STRUCTURE

When you spent time as a leadership team getting crystal clear on your Accountability Chart, you created the first essential layer of organizational accountability. No longer can people point fingers, wonder who's responsible for what, or claim confusion about roles and responsibilities.

The Accountability Chart answers fundamental questions that plague most organizations: What is the right structure for our organization as we grow? Who's accountable for what? What is each seat responsible for accomplishing? Who do we go to when we need decisions or support in specific areas?

This clarity eliminates the frustrating "who handles this?" conversations that waste everyone's time and create organizational friction. When people know exactly where to go with questions, concerns, or requests, communication becomes more efficient and effective.

Role clarity, however, is only half of the accountability equation. The other half is ensuring you have the Right People in the Right Seats—people who truly GWC (Get it, Want it, and have the Capacity to do) their roles.

When someone "Gets it," all of the neurons in their brain connect when you explain the job, and they do the work. They understand all the ins and outs of the position. When they "Want it," they genuinely want to do the job—they get up every morning wanting to do it. You can't pay, motivate, force, or beg them to want it; they have to want it on their own. When they have the "Capacity," they possess the mental, physical, spiritual, time, knowledge, and emotional capacity to do the job.

When someone Gets it, Wants it, and has the Capacity, they thrive. Missing any piece of GWC makes success nearly impossible. When you combine clear roles with people who truly GWC them, you create an environment where accountability feels natural rather than forced. People take ownership because they understand their role, genuinely want to do it, and have the capacity to succeed.

SCORECARD ACCOUNTABILITY: NUMBERS DON'T LIE

By implementing your Scorecard, you've introduced a powerful form of accountability around performance and results. You've assigned specific numbers to specific people, creating individual ownership of measurable outcomes.

Every week in your Level 10 Meetings, those people report whether their numbers are on track or off track to the goal. There's nowhere to hide when the data is visible to everyone, and there's no ambiguity about whether performance is meeting expectations.

This transparency creates healthy peer pressure—people don't want to be the one consistently reporting "off track" to their colleagues. More importantly, it helps people drive results proactively rather than waiting for someone else to tell them how they're doing.

QUARTERLY ACCOUNTABILITY THROUGH ROCKS

Your Rocks have created a powerful form of quarterly accountability that most organizations completely lack. Each Rock belongs to a specific person, with clear success criteria and completion dates.

Every week, that person reports "on track" or "off track" to the entire team. No more letting important initiatives slip through the cracks, hoping someone else will pick up the ball, or wondering why critical projects aren't getting completed.

This creates what's called "implementation intentions"— specific plans for when, where, and how goals will be achieved.

When people make specific plans about when, where, and how they'll achieve their goals, they're much more likely to actually follow through.

WEEKLY ACCOUNTABILITY THROUGH TO-DOS

During each Level 10 Meeting, you assign specific action items to specific people with specific due dates. The following week, those people report whether they are "done" or "not done" to the team. Simple, clear, and effective.

This creates a weekly cadence of commitment and follow-through that builds accountability muscles throughout your organization. People begin to take their commitments more seriously when they know they'll be asked about them publicly and regularly.

THE INTEGRATION EFFECT: LEVEL 10 MEETINGS

This is where the magic happens: Your Level 10 Meetings tie everything into one cohesive accountability system. The meeting agenda forces you to look at The Accountability Chart when issues arise—you know exactly who to turn to when numbers are off track or Rocks need support.

The cadence of weekly reporting creates a predictable drumbeat of accountability that becomes second nature rather than feeling forced or uncomfortable. Most importantly, you're doing all of this accountability work transparently and publicly. When someone reports that their number is off track or their Rock is stuck, the entire team hears it. This models the behavior you want to see throughout the organization: this is what an accountable team looks like in action.

THE PSYCHOLOGY OF PUBLIC ACCOUNTABILITY

This transparent approach to accountability is designed to create some productive discomfort. It's the mild discomfort of saying "Off Track" or "Not Done" publicly that motivates accountable people to get their Rock back on track or to complete their To-Do before the next meeting.

Similarly, people experience genuine satisfaction when they get to report "On Track" or "Done" to their colleagues. This positive reinforcement rewards the behaviors you want repeated.

In the age of technology, it may seem more efficient to look at a screen where everyone can see the status of Measurables, Rocks, and To-dos, but that approach eliminates the psychological impact that drives behavior change. Don't rob your team of this important experience—the verbal reporting is crucial to building accountability throughout your organization.

As you roll out departmental Level 10 Meetings, you're carrying that same transparency and accountability down into each department. You're not just implementing a tool—you're modeling a way of being accountable that will ripple through your entire organization systematically.

Now that your Foundational Tools are working well, two additional tools will complete your accountability foundation and strengthen your organizational discipline. These tools address the remaining gaps in how people understand what's expected of them and how they measure their individual contribution to organizational success.

3-STEP PROCESS DOCUMENTER

The 3-Step Process Documenter is an EOS tool for strengthening the Process Component. If you're working with a

Professional EOS Implementer, they'll teach the leadership team about the 3-Step Process Documenter in detail during a Quarterly session, typically once the Foundational Tools are working well.

Committing to identifying, documenting, and rolling out your Core Processes is a critical part of accountability because people need to know what's expected of them—and having clear processes is one of the best ways to set those expectations.

- **Step 1:** Identify your core processes—the 6–12 most important processes that drive your business results and customer experience.

- **Step 2:** Document and simplify each core process—not detailed step-by-step procedures, but clear workflows that show the major steps and decision points.

- **Step 3:** Package them—and make them easy to find and use.

Essentially, you're creating a playbook for your team. This is how we hire people. This is how we process claims. This is how we onboard new customers. This is how we handle invoices.

When everyone knows the "right way" to execute these critical processes, accountability becomes much easier and more objective. People can be held accountable for following established processes, and deviations can be identified and corrected quickly.

Once you've completed these three steps—identifying, documenting, and packaging your core processes—the real work begins: getting them followed by all (FBA). Having processes documented and packaged is valuable, but it doesn't create accountability or consistency until everyone actually uses them. This is where many organizations stumble—they complete the documentation work and assume the job is done, only to discover six months later that the beautifully packaged processes are gathering digital dust while people continue operating the old way.

WHAT "FOLLOWED BY ALL" REALLY MEANS

Once your core processes are identified, documented, and packaged, the next critical discipline is ensuring they are followed by all. This means more than having processes sitting in a binder or on a shared drive that nobody looks at.

Getting processes followed by all means:

- **Training** people so they understand not just what to do, but why each step matters.
- **Measuring** compliance through quality checks, audits, reports, or Measurables.
- **Managing** processes by observing work and providing feedback when people stray from them.
- **Updating** processes regularly so they remain relevant and useful as the business evolves.

Process documentation creates clear standards that make accountability conversations much more objective and productive. Instead of arguing about whether someone did something "right," you can refer to the documented process and discuss whether it is correct, needs updating, or is a training issue. This eliminates ambiguity and personal interpretation, replacing them with clear standards that everyone understands and agrees to follow.

ROLLING OUT PROCESS DOCUMENTATION

Getting your Core Processes documented and followed by all typically takes 6–12 months, and most organizations find success when they approach it strategically rather than trying to tackle everything at once.

Many leadership teams discover that timing this initiative properly makes a significant difference in adoption. Rather than introducing process documentation during your initial Rollout, you might consider waiting until Level 10 Meetings, Rocks, and Scorecards are working consistently. Your people often need time to absorb the foundational disciplines before taking on additional accountability systems.

Many organizations discover that tackling two or three processes per quarter creates manageable progress without overwhelming other business priorities. This approach gives you time to get each process working well and gather feedback before moving to the next ones.

REAL-WORLD EXAMPLE: THE COST OF INCONSISTENT PROCESSES

An established Colorado home builder struggled to complete projects on schedule while maintaining quality standards. Deadlines slipped, customer blue-tape lists grew, warranty calls increased, and profits quietly leaked away. By running the numbers, they saw that inconsistent processes were costing them more than $1 million a year. That eye-opening realization sparked a company-wide commitment to drive accountability.

Together, the leadership team and managers committed to strengthening the Process Component using the Process! Process (detailed in the EOS Mastery Series book, *Process!*, by Lisa Gonzalez and Mike Paton) and embarked on the journey to document, simplify, and get processes followed by all. With consistent training, every team member—from project managers to site supervisors—understood and applied the same standards. Within a few months, they closed the process holes that had been costing the company money, resulting in a much more peaceful and profitable life for everyone.

Rollout Planning Tip: *Many leaders underestimate the time, patience, and repetition required for teams to adopt new processes, so be sure to build this into your Rollout Plan.*

Mastery Tip: *For more detail about strengthening the Process Component, consider reading* Process! *by Lisa Gonzalez and Mike Paton, published in 2022 as part of the EOS Mastery series.*

MEASUREABLES: EVERYONE HAS A NUMBER

By this point in your EOS journey, you should have Scorecards working effectively at both the company and department levels, with five to fifteen numbers tracked weekly at each level. The next step is to ensure that everyone in the organization has at least one number they're personally accountable for keeping on track.

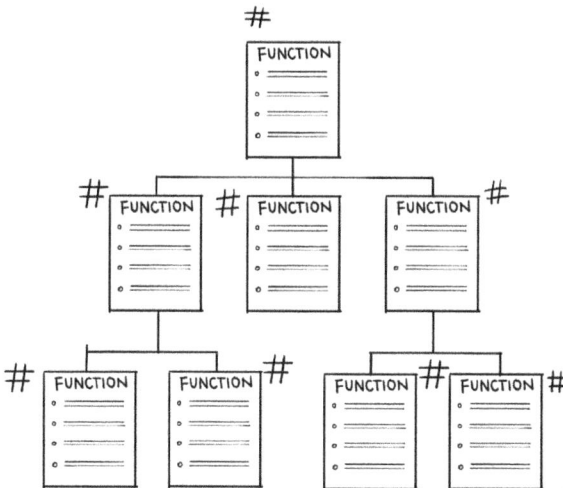

This doesn't mean every number needs to appear on a formal Scorecard that gets reviewed in meetings. Some numbers will be visible on Scorecards as weekly Measureables, while others may be more personal or specific to individual roles.

EXAMPLES OF INDIVIDUAL ACCOUNTABILITY NUMBERS

Someone might have a number like "answer phone within two rings," where their target consistently meets that standard. They know that's their number and what they're accountable for, but it doesn't necessarily need to show up on any team Scorecard.

A quality inspector might be accountable for "zero defects found in my inspection area" with weekly tracking that helps them maintain focus and pride in their work. A customer service representative might track "first-call resolution rate above 85 percent" as their personal measure of effectiveness and skill development.

INDIVIDUAL NUMBERS THAT ROLL UP TO TEAM RESULTS

Sometimes multiple people's individual numbers roll up to create a team result. There might be five people on a production team, and each person is accountable for completing $10,000 worth of work each week, which means the team collectively delivers $50,000. Everyone knows their individual number and understands how it contributes to the team's total output.

A sales team works the same way. Each salesperson has individual revenue targets, and those individual numbers add up to the team's total revenue goal. An operations team might each own a specific metric for their part of the process—one person tracks setup time, another tracks cycle time, another tracks quality checks—and together these individual numbers determine overall process performance.

Here's the essential point: if you have 100 people in your company, that doesn't mean you're tracking 100 different numbers on various Scorecards. It means that if you walked up to any of the 100 people in the company and asked, "What's your number?" they should be able to tell you immediately, without hesitation.

No deer-in-headlights looks, no "Um, let me get back to you on that," and no confusion about what they're accountable for achieving. When you reach that point—when everyone has a number they own and understand—you are genuinely strong in the Data Component.

ROLLING OUT INDIVIDUAL NUMBERS

Getting everyone in your organization to have at least one meaningful number they're accountable for often takes several quarters, and most companies find success with a thoughtful, department-by-department approach.

You may discover that many individual numbers naturally emerge from your existing leadership and departmental Scorecards. Consider looking for numbers that can be broken down by person, location, or team. Your sales team probably already has individual targets, but other departments might benefit from more creative thinking to identify meaningful metrics.

Rather than trying to assign numbers to everyone simultaneously, you might find it more effective to work with each department to brainstorm individual metrics that make sense for their specific roles. Some will be obvious, like production quotas or customer satisfaction scores. Others may require looking at outcomes rather than activities—such as response times, project completion rates, process improvement suggestions, or quality metrics.

Consider setting realistic expectations for your timeline. Depending on your organization's size and complexity, you might plan for three to six quarters to get everyone a meaningful number. Some teams set intermediate milestones, such as getting all managers' numbers by the second quarter or completing the sales and operations teams before moving to support functions.

Try not to let "hard to measure" roles slow your progress. While not every job has obvious numbers, most roles have measurable outcomes when you think creatively. Administrative roles might track processing times or accuracy rates. Project managers could own on-time delivery or budget variance. Even roles like HR can measure time-to-fill and employee retention rates.

The goal isn't to create a surveillance system; it's to help everyone understand what success looks like in their role and give them objective feedback about their performance. When people know their number and can see their progress, they often naturally take more ownership of their results.

Rollout Planning Tip: Depending on the size of your team, it can take anywhere from a few months to several quarters to get to the point where everyone has a number. Set a target for when you would like to achieve this goal and work backwards from there. Remember: Progress, not perfection!

Mastery Tip: For more depth on the Data Component, Scorecards, and everyone having a number, consider reading Data *by Mark O'Donnell, Mark Stanley, and Angela Kalemis, published in 2024 as part of the EOS Mastery series.*

LEADERSHIP + MANAGEMENT = ACCOUNTABILITY

Beyond these core accountability tools, there's one additional EOS tool that Gino Wickman calls "the icing on the cake": LMA—Leadership, Management, and Accountability. LMA is one of the 20 EOS Tools in the EOS Toolbox, and it represents the number one role in any seat on the Accountability Chart that has direct reports. If you have LMA in your seat, you have a responsibility to lead, manage, and create an environment of accountability on your team.

$$L + M = A$$

If you're working with a Professional EOS Implementer, they'll teach the leadership team about LMA in detail during a Quarterly session, typically once the Foundational Tools are working well. If you're implementing EOS on your own, you can learn about LMA through the book *How to Be a Great Boss* by Gino Wickman and René Boer, which provides extensive detail about creating an environment of accountability through great leadership and management.

Here's what you need to know: LMA consists of five leadership practices and five management practices. Together, these ten practices help anyone with direct reports create an environment of accountability on their team.

We won't dive deep into these practices in this book—that's what *How to Be a Great Boss* is for. As you implement EOS, everyone in your organization with direct reports should learn this content.

REAL-WORLD EXAMPLE: ELEVATING MANAGERS TO CREATE LEADERSHIP CAPACITY

At Konrady Plastics, a family-owned manufacturer in Portage, Indiana, the leadership team faced a problem that plagues countless growing businesses: they couldn't find time to work *on* the business because they were drowning *in* it.

The leadership team recognized they needed to fundamentally change how the company operated. They identified high-potential team members who could be elevated into mid-management positions—people who had both the capability and desire to take on greater responsibility. In doing so, they found some team members hesitant and unsure if being a manager was the right position for them, and they found others who thought they understood what was required to lead and manage, but at times struggled to either manage or lead. Then they brought in their EOS Implementer to conduct an LMA training session to create alignment with emerging leaders and provide them with the skills needed to truly own their areas of responsibility: setting clear expectations, holding people accountable, solving problems at their level, and making decisions confidently.

Over the following quarters, something important became clear: not everyone wanted to—or could—step into these leadership roles. Some team members embraced the challenge, growing into their expanded responsibilities with enthusiasm. Others, despite the training and support, either weren't interested in the added accountability or simply weren't capable of making the leap. The real differentiator wasn't just management capability—it was the ability to take on full ownership of the role and the willingness to be personally accountable and hold their team members accountable for outcomes, not just tasks.

The leadership team made the tough but necessary decisions to ensure they had the right people in the right seats—people who would embrace true accountability. This was the breakthrough. Quarter by quarter, as these mid-managers took ownership of daily operations and their results, the leadership team found themselves gradually freed from the tactical firefighting that had consumed their days. They could finally let go because they knew things would get done without their constant oversight and involvement. Today, they spend more of their time doing what leaders should do: thinking strategically, planning for growth, and steering the company toward its long-term vision.

"Things feel more peaceful now," reflects Leah Konrady, Co-Owner & Visionary. "We're spending less time firefighting, and more time thinking strategically about how to grow the company."

Remember, accountability isn't about catching people doing things wrong. It's about creating crystal-clear expectations and then helping people meet them. It's about building a culture where people hold themselves accountable because they care about the outcome, not because they're afraid of getting in trouble.

Rollout Planning Tip: *Consider introducing LMA concepts after Foundational Tools are working well, typically six to nine months into Rollout. There's only so much change people can absorb at once.*

THE ART OF LETTING GO

Remember in Chapter 4 when we discussed the shift from student to teacher and the need to "let go of the vine"? The control issues that make leaders hesitant to begin rollout are the same ones that prevent them from creating sustainable accountability.

At the beginning of every EOS Client Journey, we spend considerable time discussing the concept of "letting go of the vine." There's a story in *Traction* about an entrepreneur who struggles with this concept—it usually generates knowing laughter from leadership teams because everyone recognizes themselves in this "fictional" character.[6]

Here's the uncomfortable truth that many leaders face: letting go is terrifying because it means releasing direct control over outcomes that feel critically important. Many leadership team members harbor a deep fear that if they aren't personally involved in every detail, their department—or the entire company—will be driven straight into a ditch.

This fear is often amplified by ego and compounded by the reality that many leaders don't fully trust their people yet (often due to unresolved GWC issues they haven't addressed). When you combine control needs with trust issues, Rollout failure becomes almost inevitable.

The connection to accountability is critical: true accountability can only exist when people have the freedom to own their results. If you're micromanaging every decision and hovering over every task, you're not creating accountability; you're creating dependency.

WHY CONTROL KILLS ROLLOUT

You simply cannot scale EOS through control and micromanagement. It's like trying to conduct an orchestra by playing every instrument yourself—exhausting, ineffective, and ultimately impossible as the organization grows.

What separates thriving organizations from struggling ones: great leaders understand that their job isn't to control everything; it's to create more leaders throughout the organization. Your next-level leaders aren't just implementers of your vision; they're the multipliers who will exponentially expand EOS throughout your organization.

The magic happens when you stop asking, "How do I make sure this gets done right?" and start asking, "How do I develop leaders who can make this happen better than I could?" That fundamental shift in mindset transforms not just your Rollout, but your entire approach to leadership and organizational development.

This doesn't mean abandoning accountability or accepting mediocre results. It means building systems and developing people so that high performance becomes sustainable and scalable rather than dependent on your direct involvement.

Rollout Planning Tip: *Leadership team members don't need to be perfectly executing the 5 Leadership and 5 Management Best Practices before they start teaching LMA to your next-level leaders. In fact, it's often more effective if leadership team members exhibit vulnerability and share where they are working to improve. LMA Mastery is a lifelong journey.*

Mastery Tip: *For more depth on LMA, consider reading* How to Be a Great Boss *by Gino Wickman and René Boer, published in 2018 as part of The Traction Library® series.*

A CULTURE OF ACCOUNTABILITY

When you create an environment of accountability at the leadership level, something incredible happens: it spreads. Your people see how the leadership team operates—how you report on your numbers honestly, how you admit when you're off track on a Rock, how you follow through on your To-Dos. They start to model that behavior in their own teams.

Pretty soon, accountability isn't something you have to enforce—it's simply how your organization operates. People take ownership naturally. They solve problems proactively. They communicate openly when they're struggling instead of hoping no one will notice.

This is what separates good organizations from great ones. Great organizations don't just have accountability systems; they have accountability cultures. And that culture starts with you and the leadership team showing everyone else what real accountability looks like.

You're not just implementing tools. You're transforming the way your organization operates. Keep going.

Rollout Tool: *Ready to check your progress? The INTEGRATION section of your Rollout Tracker will show you what's solid and what still needs work.*

Rollout Tool: *Running into challenges? The Rollout Troubleshooting Guide in Appendix D addresses the 10 most common Rollout issues with specific symptoms, root causes, and solutions.*

CHAPTER 9 SUMMARY

Your foundational EOS tools have created the structural foundation for accountability. Completing this foundation with process documentation, individual Measurables, and leadership development (LMA) creates an environment where accountability feels natural rather than forced.

Key elements that complete your accountability foundation:

- **Clear Structure** through your Accountability Chart eliminates confusion about roles and responsibilities.
- **Transparent Performance** through Scorecards, Rocks, and Level 10 Meetings creates healthy peer pressure and ownership.

- **Process Documentation** through the 3-Step Process Documenter creates alignment about the "right" way to execute core activities.

- **Individual Ownership** through ensuring everyone has a Measurable creates personal accountability at every level.

- **LMA** helps managers create accountability in their teams through great leadership and management.

You've built a comprehensive accountability system that enables people to take ownership and drive results consistently. Your EOS Foundational Tools are working, the vision is integrated into daily operations, and your culture supports high performance. Now comes the ultimate test: making sure all these changes and improvements stick. The difference between organizations that sustain EOS success and those that gradually drift back to old habits lies in their commitment to treating EOS as a permanent operating system rather than a temporary improvement program.

What's Next: In Chapter 10, we'll explore how to sustain EOS in the long term by building sustainability, measuring results, and maintaining momentum amid inevitable changes and challenges.

REFLECTION QUESTIONS

1. **Core Processes**: Are we ready to identify, simplify, and document our 6-12 Core Processes using the 3-Step Process Documenter? Once we do that, how will we ensure that our processes are consistently followed by everyone? How much time should we allocate in our Rollout plan for completing these activities?

2. **Measurables (Everyone Has a Number):** Are we ready to clarify individual expectations and ensure everyone has a number they are accountable for keeping track of? How long do we think it will take to reach a point where everyone in the organization has a number?

3. **Letting Go of the Vine**: What specific areas are we holding onto too tightly out of fear, and how is our need for control potentially preventing people from taking true ownership of their results? Are there unresolved GWC issues holding us back?

4. **LMA**: Are we ready to learn about the Five Leadership Practices and Five Management Practices? When should we plan to read How to Be a Great Boss as a leadership team? When will we introduce this content to our mid-managers?

10

RUNNING ON EOS...FOREVER

A goal is a dream with a deadline.
But commitment is what transforms the
dream of today into the reality of tomorrow.

—Donna Shalala

"*You know, there's 'work' in work,*" as one of our mentors, René Boer, often reminds us. This simple truth captures the essence of what separates great organizations from good ones. The truth about sustaining EOS success is both sobering and exciting: Maintaining 80 percent strength across the Six Key Components requires unwavering discipline and intentional effort that never truly ends.

You've successfully moved through Preparation, Launch, and Integration. Now comes the Sustainability phase—making EOS your permanent operating system.

You've built a strong accountability foundation with the five EOS Foundational Tools, process documentation, and individual Measurables. Your people understand expectations, report transparently, and take ownership of results. And now comes the real test: making this stick forever.

We've seen countless leadership teams return for "tune-ups" or "reboots" because they gradually lost focus on EOS fundamentals over time. When Level 10 Meetings start happening sporadically, when the V/TO begins gathering dust, when Rocks aren't prioritized, when Scorecards stop driving decisions, the organizational slide is swift and unmistakable.

What sets the EOS virtuosos apart is their ongoing commitment to operational excellence. They understand that EOS is an operating system that runs underneath everything they do—not a program they use occasionally. They trust the EOS Process, rely on the EOS tools, and are committed to running on EOS... forever.

Here's the key insight that makes this possible: **EOS is a process.** And like any process, it only works when it's followed by all. The secret to running on EOS forever isn't perfect implementation or flawless execution—it's getting everyone in your organization to use the EOS tools consistently, day after day, week after week, quarter after quarter, year after year.

Rollout Tool: Running into challenges? The Rollout Troubleshooting Guide in Appendix D addresses the 10 most common Rollout issues with specific symptoms, root causes, and solutions.

THE CHOIR THAT NEVER STOPS PRACTICING

Think of it like a world-class choir preparing for a performance. Individual singers might have beautiful voices, but the magic happens when everyone commits to following the conductor, staying in tempo, and blending their voices in harmony. A choir where some members haven't learned their notes or skip practice sessions when it's inconvenient doesn't just sound mediocre—it sounds chaotic.

What distinguishes amateur choirs from professional ones: professional choirs never stop practicing. They don't declare victory after one beautiful performance and assume they can coast on past success. They understand that excellence requires ongoing commitment to the fundamentals, season after season, year after year.

The same principle applies to running on EOS. You might have talented people and good intentions, but organizational harmony only emerges when everyone follows EOS together, maintains the same discipline, and stays in tune with each other—not just this quarter, but every quarter.

This shows up in very practical ways. When a customer crisis arises during your Level 10 Meeting, do you cancel the meeting to address it, or do you use the meeting structure to address it systematically? When business is booming, and everything feels under control, do you maintain your quarterly planning discipline, or do you skip it because "we don't need it right now"?

These small choices compound into dramatically different outcomes over time—just like a choir where individual choices and voices determine whether the audience hears harmony or chaos.

THE CONDUCTOR'S ONGOING ROLE

Even the most accomplished choir needs consistent conducting to maintain excellence over time. Similarly, sustaining EOS requires ongoing orchestration—someone who maintains or changes the tempo, notices when departments start drifting out of sync, and keeps everyone focused on playing their part in the larger composition.

This is often where the Rollout Champion's conductor-like qualities are most valuable in the long term. Whether that's the Integrator or another leader who took on this role, they're positioned to see patterns across the organization, identify where additional training or support is needed, and ensure that the discipline of following EOS doesn't fade when business pressures mount.

The key is ensuring someone maintains this orchestrating perspective—it may continue to be the same person who led your initial Rollout, or the responsibility may naturally shift to another leader as your organization matures with EOS.

Just as a conductor never stops listening for harmony and tempo, your ongoing EOS champion never stops monitoring whether EOS is being followed by all. This brings us to the heart of sustainability: the specific disciplines that keep EOS alive in your organization.

GETTING EOS FOLLOWED BY ALL

In Chapter 9, we introduced the 3-Step Process Documenter and explored what it means to get processes "followed by all." You learned that documenting a process is only the beginning—the real challenge is ensuring everyone follows it consistently. That same principle applies here, but now we're talking about the most essential process of all: EOS itself.

EOS is a process, and the key to running on EOS forever is getting EOS followed by all (FBA). When everyone follows the EOS Process consistently, you create the organizational discipline that helps you make your vision a reality.

Like any process, getting EOS followed by all requires mastering four critical disciplines that work together in a continuous loop: Train → Measure → Manage → Update

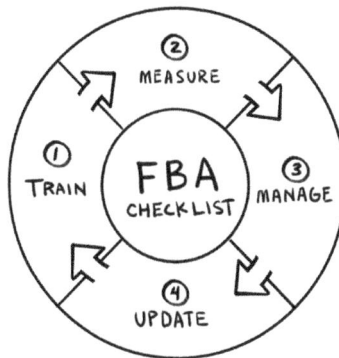

Each discipline supports the others. Training equips your team to use EOS correctly. Measuring shows whether they're actually using it. Managing addresses gaps when people drift from the disciplines. And updating keeps everything relevant as your organization evolves. Together, these four disciplines make EOS stick.

Let's explore each discipline, starting with training—because your ongoing commitment to developing EOS competency determines whether it becomes your permanent operating system or just another program that fades away.

TRAINING: AN ONGOING COMMITMENT

Training isn't something you do during Rollout and then discontinue. It's an ongoing commitment to developing EOS competency at every level so that everyone can follow EOS effectively. As your company evolves, new people join who have never experienced EOS. Departments shift and grow. Leaders at every level need reinforcement and support to maintain their commitment to following EOS.

Level 10 Meetings. Every Level 10 Meeting is a training opportunity. When you consistently demonstrate EOS discipline in these weekly sessions, you're teaching by example. Your commitment to the Meeting Pulse, IDS methodology, and Scorecard discipline models what you expect throughout the organization. The discipline you demonstrate in staying on track, asking the right questions, and driving toward solutions teaches your team more about following EOS than any formal training session could.

Issues Solving Track. Don't assume people naturally know how to identify issues, discuss them productively, and solve them at the root level. Invest time in teaching IDS methodology using the Issues Solving Track (see *Traction*, Chapter 6), practicing it together, and celebrating when teams apply it effectively.

Quarterly State of the Company Meetings. Every quarter, forever, stand in front of your organization and report honestly on your progress, challenges, and plans for the future. This isn't something you do until people "understand" EOS and then discontinue. This quarterly meeting cadence creates a powerful cycle of public commitment, focused execution, and transparent reporting that drives everyone to follow EOS throughout the organization.

Departmental Quarterlies and Annuals. Your teams need regular reinforcement of EOS principles and tools, as well as regular reminders of where you are going as an organization. Use these sessions to celebrate successes, address challenges, and strengthen their understanding of how EOS will help you achieve your vision.

Onboarding Integration. Every new person who joins your organization needs to understand your vision and EOS. Don't assume they'll absorb information through osmosis. Integrate EOS orientation into your onboarding process for all new hires, with a particular focus on those joining the leadership team.

Community Learning and Connection. Stay connected to the broader EOS community through ongoing learning and development opportunities. Send your champions and key leaders to the EOS Conference, or encourage them to participate in EOS peer groups and other learning opportunities to deepen their skills and maintain momentum.

MEASUREMENT: TRACKING SUCCESS

You can't manage what you don't measure. Tracking things systematically gives you the objective data you need to see where EOS is working well and where people may need more support.

Compliance: Are the Tools Being Used as Designed? Regular EOS tool reviews can help you identify where discipline has slipped or where additional training is needed. Look for warning signs, such as incomplete Scorecards, poorly written Rocks, or Level 10 Meetings that consistently run over time.

Just as you measure business results, you must also measure how well the EOS principles are being followed. The tools only work when they're used correctly and consistently.

Outcomes: Are You Getting Results? The most important measures of success are results-based.

- **Level 10 Meeting Ratings**: Aim for an average of 8.75+ across all teams. Lower ratings indicate process issues that need attention.

- **To-Do Completion Rate**: 90+ percent of To-dos should be completed every week.

- **Rock Completion Rate**: Target 80+ percent quarterly Rock completion as your Rock-setting and execution skills mature.

- **Annual Goal Completion Rate**: Aim for 80+ percent Goal completion as your planning and execution skills become more effective.

- **Organizational Checkup:** Administer this assessment periodically (at least once per year) to smoke out issues and assess your strength in the Six Key Components of the EOS Model. A score of 80 percent or better is the target.

Rollout Planning Tip: Consider how often you will use the Organizational Checkup to evaluate the progress you are making toward 80+ percent strength in the Six Key Components of the EOS Model, and build it into your Rollout Plan

Mastery Tip: Use the online version of the Organizational Checkup to send the assessment out to your entire organization and get your results in a comprehensive report. Visit OrganizationalCheckup.com to create a free company account.

MANAGEMENT: LEADING OTHERS TO FOLLOW EOS

Measurement without management is just data collection. Getting EOS followed by all requires leaders who consistently demonstrate the behaviors they expect from others, especially when pressure mounts or when it would be easier to revert to old habits.

Provide Clear Direction. Your people need to understand not just what to do, but why following EOS matters and how their work contributes to organizational success. This clarity stems from consistently communicating your vision and priorities. Your V/TO isn't a document you create once—it's a communication tool you use constantly to maintain alignment and focus.

Set Clear Expectations. Be explicit about what success looks like for individuals and teams in your organization. Don't assume people understand your expectations. Communicate standards clearly and hold people accountable consistently.

Provide Necessary Resources. Make sure your teams have the training, resources, and empowerment they need to succeed. Don't set people up for failure by expecting them to follow EOS without providing the support systems that make it possible.

Let Go of the Vine. As a leader, you must resist the temptation to jump in and solve every problem yourself. Trust your people to use the EOS tools and methodology, even when they're still learning. Your job is to coach and develop, not to rescue. Create independence, not dependence.

Connect the Dots. When you face difficult decisions, show your team how you apply your core values, consider the vision, and use data to inform your decisions. Your actions speak louder than your words about your commitment to following EOS.

Take Regular Clarity Breaks. Schedule regular time to step back and assess how EOS is working for you. Are you getting the results you expected? Where do you need to adjust your approach? These reflection periods prevent drift and maintain focus on consistently using EOS tools and disciplines to achieve your vision.

Protect The Meeting Pulse. Don't cancel or shorten Level 10 Meetings, Quarterlies, or Annuals for "more urgent" matters. Your commitment to the Meeting Pulse sets the standard for the entire organization. If leaders treat these meetings as optional, everyone else will too.

UPDATING: CONTINUOUS IMPROVEMENT AND ADAPTATION

EOS isn't a static system; it's a living framework that should evolve as your organization grows and learns. Regular updates keep your tools sharp and strengthen your commitment to following EOS disciplines.

Build a Culture of Continuous Improvement. Systematic assessment and adjustment should be built into your EOS implementation. What's working well? What needs refinement? How can you simplify or strengthen your processes based on experience? Focus on progress, not perfection.

Evolve Your EOS Tools. EOS tools are intended to be reviewed and referenced continuously. They are not set-it-and-forget-it items. Always think, "There's a tool for that!" As you learn what works in your specific context, update your tools accordingly.

- The V/TO will evolve as your vision gets clearer.
- Rocks will get updated every quarter, and you'll set new 1-Year Goals annually.
- Your Accountability Chart should be continuously updated as your business evolves.
- Your Meeting Pulse may need to change as your department structures evolve.
- Your Scorecard and Measurables may need to be simplified or adjusted as you grow.
- Processes should be updated regularly as your business changes.

KEEP RAISING THE BAR

As you deepen your understanding of EOS over the years, your definition of what 80 percent strong actually looks like will continue to evolve. What feels like strong execution in your second year of EOS might look quite different from your perspective in year five. This isn't a failure of your earlier efforts; it's evidence of genuine mastery developing over time.

REAL-WORLD EXAMPLE: A DECADE OF EOS MASTERY

When Total Security Solutions began their EOS journey, they were a 25-person company with $8 million in revenue and an owner, Jim Richards, wearing multiple hats without a true leadership team. Jim's ambitious 10-Year Target seemed almost impossible: Reach $20 million by 2020.

Then something remarkable happened. By building a leadership team and implementing EOS systematically, TSS reached $20 million in revenue by 2017—three years ahead of schedule. Rather than celebrating and coasting, they reset their sights higher: $50 million by 2027.

Their EOS discipline only deepened from there. They rolled out Level 10 Meetings across the organization, built comprehensive Scorecards for each team, and established quarterly Rocks throughout the organization. Not every quarter was perfect—sometimes numbers were missed, Rocks weren't completed, and initiatives stalled. Each time they stumbled, they used their quarterly reflection to identify what went wrong and how to improve.

"Some quarters were 'winning' quarters, others were 'learning' quarters," Jim explains. "Both were valuable for building our EOS mastery."

They also began measuring their organizational strength using the Organizational Checkup, striving to maintain scores above 80 percent and making systematic adjustments when they fell short. This discipline of honest assessment and continuous improvement became part of their company's DNA.

When TSS hit $50 million in 2024—three years early again—they didn't slow down. They set an even bolder vision: $250 million by 2035.

Today, Total Security Solutions demonstrates what "running on EOS forever" actually looks like. Every new employee receives a copy of *What the Heck is EOS?* and completes comprehensive vision and EOS training, and all managers attend LMA training through their *How to Be a Great Boss* book club. Their Core Values, Core Focus, 3 Uniques, and Proven Process are visible throughout their facilities, guiding every customer interaction and business decision.

EOS isn't something they do; it's how they operate. "We're committed to getting 1 percent better every day," Jim reflects. "EOS gives us the framework to make that improvement systematic rather than random. I used to feel like the responsibility for achieving our vision rested entirely on my shoulders. Now, I'm surrounded by people who are just as excited about where we're going, and I know we can get there—together."

That's what a decade of EOS mastery looks like: not perfection, but relentless commitment to the disciplines that create sustainable excellence.

Just as a musician's understanding of a piece deepens with years of practice, your organization's sophistication with EOS will continue growing. The Level 10 Meetings that felt smooth and effective in year two might reveal new opportunities for depth and precision as your team's skills mature. The accountability conversations that once felt challenging become natural, creating space to focus on more nuanced aspects of leadership and team development.

This rising bar is actually a sign of success, not something to be frustrated by. It means your team is developing genuine competency rather than just going through the motions.

ENJOY THE JOURNEY

Your EOS journey continues. Your commitment deepens. Your results multiply.

This is how you run on EOS forever—not through perfect implementation, but through relentless commitment to getting EOS followed by all through systematic training, disciplined measurement, consistent management, and ongoing adaptation.

The path to running on EOS is clear. The tools are proven. The only question remaining is this: **Are you committed to getting EOS followed by all...forever?**

Your organization's future depends on your answer. Your people are counting on your leadership. Your competitors hope you'll take shortcuts or lose your commitment.

Don't let your people down. Don't take shortcuts. Don't stop following EOS. And don't forget to enjoy the journey, and have a little fun along the way!

Remember those five frustrations we started with—lack of control, people issues, profit struggles, hitting the ceiling, and nothing working? They don't have to be your story anymore.

THE FIVE FRUSTRATIONS: SOLVED

CONTROL   PEOPLE   PROFIT   CEILING   TRACTION

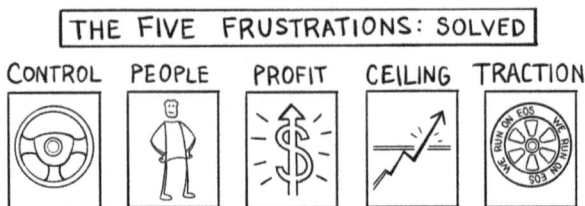

The rewards—for you, your team, and everyone your organization serves—are worth every bit of effort required to get EOS followed by all…forever.

Rollout Tool: *Now that you are in the SUSTAINABILITY phase, remember to periodically review all sections of the Rollout Tracker to ensure that your commitment to EOS stays strong.*

CHAPTER 10 SUMMARY

Running on EOS forever isn't about a perfect implementation; it's about getting EOS consistently followed by all. EOS is a process, and like any process, it only works when everyone follows it day after day, week after week, quarter after quarter, year after year. This is how you achieve your vision, maintain 80+ percent strength in the Six Key Components, and get what you want from your business.

The key to sustained success lies in mastering four critical disciplines that work together in a continuous loop:

- **Train:** Develop ongoing EOS competency through Level 10 Meetings, The Issues Solving Track, State of the Company meetings, departmental planning, comprehensive onboarding, and community learning.

- **Measure:** Track both compliance (are tools being used correctly?) and outcomes (Level 10 Meeting ratings, Rock completion rates, goal achievement, and Organizational Checkup scores).

- **Manage**: Lead by example through clear direction, proper resources, accountability, and protecting the Meeting Pulse—especially when pressure mounts.

- **Update**: Continuously improve your tools and processes as your organization grows and learns, focusing on progress over perfection.

Remember that following EOS gets easier and more natural over time, but it never becomes optional. The organizations that commit to getting EOS followed by all create predictable performance, faster decision-making, higher engagement, and sustainable growth that becomes their fundamental competitive advantage.

Your journey to running on EOS forever represents more than implementing business tools—it's about creating an organization where clarity replaces confusion, and shared purpose drives everything you do together. As you commit to this path, remember that the goal isn't perfection but consistent progress toward the vision that inspired you to begin this journey in the first place. Enjoy the journey!

REFLECTION QUESTIONS

1. **Honestly assess your current commitment**: When pressure mounts or when EOS feels inconvenient, does our leadership team double down on the disciplines or make exceptions? What does this tell us about our true commitment level?

2. **Evaluate your "followed by all" reality**: Where in our organization do we see strong EOS discipline, and

where do we see people picking and choosing which tools to follow? What specific actions will we take to address the gaps?

3. **Review the four disciplines of FBA**: Which of the four disciplines (Train, Measure, Manage, Update) is strongest in our organization? Which needs the most attention? What's our plan to strengthen the weakest area?

4. **Make your commitment clear**: What would our organization look like if everyone consistently followed EOS? Are we truly committed to getting EOS followed by all…forever?

Rollout Tool: Ready to put it all together? The complete Rollout Reflection Guide in Appendix C contains all chapter reflection questions in one place for leadership team planning sessions. You can also download the Rollout Reflection Guide from RolloutBook.com

CONCLUSION

The way I see it, if you want the rainbow,
you gotta put up with the rain.

—Dolly Parton

The Rollout journey you've embarked upon isn't just about implementing tools or following processes. It's about creating something extraordinary: an organization where clarity replaces confusion, alignment replaces conflict, and accountability replaces excuses.

Your Rollout may have started with uncertainty, resistance, or confusion. That's completely normal and expected. Change is hard, even when it's clearly beneficial. Through it all, with patience, consistency, and commitment to the principles outlined in this book, you've been building something that will serve your organization for years to come.

Think about where you started:

- A leadership team that was aligned on paper but not always in practice
- Employees who worked hard but weren't always sure how their efforts connected to something bigger

- Meetings that consumed time without always producing results
- Priorities that shifted frequently, creating frustration and wasted energy
- Accountability that felt forced rather than natural

Now consider where you are or where you're heading:

- A leadership team that speaks with one voice and models the behaviors they expect
- Employees who understand their role in achieving a compelling vision
- Meetings that drive real decisions and solve important problems
- Priorities that remain clear and focused quarter after quarter
- Accountability that feels supportive and motivating rather than punitive

This transformation didn't happen overnight, and it didn't happen by accident. It happened because you committed to a systematic approach to organizational excellence and had the patience to see it through.

Organizational excellence, like musical mastery, is never truly finished. There are always new pieces to learn, new challenges to master, and new levels of sophistication to achieve. This ongoing evolution isn't a burden; it's what keeps the work interesting, engaging, and meaningful.

The organizations that thrive over decades embrace this continuous improvement mindset, understanding that EOS isn't a destination but a better way of traveling together.

LIVING THE EOS LIFE

The journey to 100 percent strength in all Six Key Components is never truly complete—100 percent strong represents UTOPIA, an ideal state worth striving toward but rarely achieved in its entirety.

If you can consistently reach and maintain the 80 percent range across all components—and keep your organization performing at that level—that's not just a pretty great place to be. That's organizational excellence that most companies never experience.

That's when you're genuinely living what we call The EOS Life.

- **Doing what you love.** Working in a seat that you truly GWC, staying focused in your company's sweet spot rather than being pulled in countless directions.

- **With people you love.** Surrounded by colleagues who share your core values and are committed to the same vision of success, working with customers who appreciate what you have to offer.

- **Making a huge difference.** Achieving your 10-Year Target and making a meaningful dent in the universe through your collective efforts.

- **Being compensated appropriately.** Running an efficient, profitable organization that rewards everyone fairly for their contributions.

- **With time for other passions.** Creating space for family, faith, hobbies, travel, golf, knitting, model trains, music... or whatever brings you joy outside of work.

And that's entrepreneurial utopia—not a fantasy, but an achievable reality for organizations that commit to the disciplined implementation of EOS principles.

Mastery Tip: The EOS Life *by Gino Wickman will show you everything you need to live your ideal life, a life that is absolutely achievable and 100 percent customizable uniquely for you. Available in The Traction Library.*

THE JOURNEY CONTINUES

As we conclude this guide, remember that your EOS journey isn't ending; it's reaching a new level of maturity and sophistication. The tools you've learned, the disciplines you've developed, and the culture you've created will continue to evolve and improve.

New team members will join your organization and learn to contribute to the culture and vision you've created. New challenges will arise that test your systems and require adaptation. New opportunities will emerge that allow you to apply EOS principles in expanded ways.

Through all of these changes, the fundamental principles remain constant: clarity about vision, alignment around priorities, discipline in execution, and accountability for results. These principles will serve you well regardless of what the future brings.

THE SOUND OF SUCCESS

The choir metaphor we began with isn't just a metaphor; it's a promise and a prediction. With the right preparation, clear direction, sustained practice, and commitment to excellence, your organization can achieve that same kind of harmony.

Everyone working together, supporting each other, creating something far more beautiful and meaningful than any individual could produce alone. Each person plays their part skillfully while remaining connected to the larger composition. The whole becomes genuinely greater than the sum of its parts.

That's the power of a successful EOS Rollout. That's the promise of getting everyone in your organization rowing in the same direction. That's the sound of organizational excellence.

And that sound—the sound of clarity, alignment, accountability, and shared success—is music to everyone's ears.

APPENDICES

APPENDIX A:
ROLLOUT TRACKER

The Rollout Tracker helps you track your progress through the four phases of EOS Rollout: Preparation, Launch, Integration, and Sustainability. Use this tool to establish your baseline, identify gaps, and measure improvement over time.

ROLLOUT TRACKER:

GET YOUR ENTIRE TEAM RUNNING ON EOS®

Rollout equips your entire team with the tools they need to help you achieve your vision. Fully implementing EOS requires leadership team mastery, a clear plan, and commitment to make it stick. Every organization is different, so develop a Rollout plan that's right for you.

HOW TO USE THIS TRACKER:

- Establish Your Baseline: Complete this assessment before beginning your Rollout to see where you are today
- Update Regularly: Return to it periodically to measure progress
- Identify Next Steps: Use your "NO" answers to identify what needs attention next

ANSWER YES OR NO TO EACH ITEM BELOW BASED ON WHERE YOU ARE TODAY:

1. PREPARATION: THE LEADERSHIP TEAM IS READY FOR ROLLOUT ☐YES ☐NO

- Align and get ready to communicate the 5 EOS Foundational Tools™ (V/TO®, The Accountability Chart®, Rocks, The Meeting Pulse®, and Scorecard)
- Create Rollout Plan (Timeline, Roles & Responsibilities, Communication, etc.)

2. LAUNCH: THE LEADERSHIP TEAM HAS INTRODUCED THE VISION AND EOS ☐YES ☐NO

- Introduce your EOS Foundational Tools (context + content) to the organization
    - V/TO: Deliver the Core Values Speech and review each section
    - The Accountability Chart: Share the structure, functions, and roles
    - Rocks: Share your Company Rocks for the next quarter
    - The Meeting Pulse: Explain Level 10 Meetings, Quarterlies, and Annuals
    - Scorecard: Explain the importance of data and measurables
- Hand out a copy of What the Heck is EOS? to everyone
- Plan your next Quarterly State of the Company meeting to share:
    - Where we've been
    - Where we are
    - Where we're going

3. INTEGRATION: EOS TOOLS AND DISCIPLINES ARE FULLY INTEGRATED COMPANY-WIDE ☐YES ☐NO

- Departments:
    - Meet regularly using the Level 10 Meeting Agenda
    - Meet quarterly to review the Company V/TO and Departmental Plan, set Departmental and Individual Rocks, and solve issues
    - Meet annually to review the Company V/TO, update the Departmental Plan (Goals and Rocks), and solve issues
- Core Processes are documented, simplified, and Followed by All (FBA)
- Everyone has at least one number they are accountable for keeping on track
- Leaders and Managers:
    - Use Core Values to hire, fire, review, reward, and recognize
    - Have read How to Be a Great Boss and understand LMA
    - Are answering YES to the Leadership & Management Self-Assessments
    - Are holding Quarterly Conversations with direct reports

4. SUSTAINABILITY: THE LEADERSHIP TEAM IS COMMITTED TO RUNNING ON EOS...FOREVER ☐YES ☐NO

- Deliver a State of the Company every quarter
- Achieve and maintain 80%+ on the Organizational Checkup®
    - Annually as a Leadership Team
    - Annually (or quarterly, if preferred) as an entire organization
- Complete 80%+ of Goals every year
- Complete 80%+ of Rocks every quarter
- Complete 90%+ of To-Dos weekly

APPENDIX B:
ORGANIZATIONAL CHECKUP®

The Organizational Checkup measures the strength of your organization across the Six Key Components of the EOS Model: Vision, People, Data, Issues, Process, and Traction. Remember, the goal is to achieve and maintain a score of at least 80 percent—indicating that you are 80+ percent strong in the Six Key Components.

HOW TO USE THIS TOOL

Initial Baseline

- Complete this assessment as a leadership team.
- For each statement, rate your business on a scale of 1 to 5, where 1 is weak and 5 is strong.
- Calculate your total score. Most organizations score 30–60 percent when starting—this is your baseline.

During Rollout/Ongoing Use

- Complete at least twice per year as a leadership team to measure your progress.
- Target: Achieve and maintain 80+ percent.

- Identify gaps by reviewing statements your team scored 3 or below.

- Expand beyond the leadership team: Survey your entire organization annually or quarterly.

For more information on how to use the Organizational Checkup, see Chapter 10 of Traction.

ORGANIZATIONAL CHECKUP®

FOR EACH STATEMENT BELOW, RANK YOUR BUSINESS ON A SCALE OF 1 TO 5 WHERE 1 IS WEAK AND 5 IS STRONG.

		1	2	3	4	5
1.	We have a clear vision in writing that has been properly communicated and is shared by everyone in the company.	☐	☐	☐	☐	☐
2.	Our Core Values are clear, and we hire, fire, review, reward, and recognize around them.	☐	☐	☐	☐	☐
3.	Our Core Focus (core business) is clear, and we keep our people, systems, and processes aligned and focused on it.	☐	☐	☐	☐	☐
4.	Our 10-Year Target (big, long-range business goal) is clear, communicated regularly, and is shared by all.	☐	☐	☐	☐	☐
5.	Our target market (definition of our ideal customer) is clear, and all of our marketing and sales efforts are focused on it.	☐	☐	☐	☐	☐
6.	Our 3 Uniques (differentiators) are clear, and all of our marketing and sales efforts communicate them.	☐	☐	☐	☐	☐
7.	We have a proven process for doing business with our customers. It has been named and visually illustrated, and all of our salespeople use it.	☐	☐	☐	☐	☐
8.	All of the people in our organization are the "right people" (they fit our culture and share our Core Values).	☐	☐	☐	☐	☐
9.	Our Accountability Chart (organizational chart that includes roles/responsibilities) is clear, complete, and constantly updated.	☐	☐	☐	☐	☐
10.	Everyone is in the "right seat" (they "get it, want it, and have the capacity to do their jobs well").	☐	☐	☐	☐	☐
11.	Our leadership team is open and honest and demonstrates a high level of trust.	☐	☐	☐	☐	☐
12.	Everyone has Rocks (1 to 7 priorities per quarter) and is focused on them.	☐	☐	☐	☐	☐

ORGANIZATIONAL CHECKUP

	1	2	3	4	5
13. Everyone is engaged in a regular Meeting Pulse (weekly, quarterly, annually).	☐	☐	☐	☐	☐
14. All meetings are on the same day and at the same time, have the same agenda, start on time, and end on time.	☐	☐	☐	☐	☐
15. All teams clearly identify, discuss, and solve issues for the long-term greater good of the company.	☐	☐	☐	☐	☐
16. Our Core Processes are documented, simplified, and Followed By All to consistently produce the results we want.	☐	☐	☐	☐	☐
17. We have systems for receiving regular feedback from customers and employees, so we always know their level of satisfaction.	☐	☐	☐	☐	☐
18. A Scorecard(s) for tracking weekly metrics/measurables is in place to consistently predict that we are on track to achieve the results we want.	☐	☐	☐	☐	☐
19. Everyone in the organization has at least one number they are accountable for keeping on track each week.	☐	☐	☐	☐	☐
20. We have a budget and are monitoring it regularly (e.g., monthly or quarterly).	☐	☐	☐	☐	☐
Total number of each ranking	☐	☐	☐	☐	☐
	x1	x2	x3	x4	x5
Multiply by the number above	☐	☐	☐	☐	☐

Add all five numbers to determine the percentage score that reflects the current state of your company:

☐ %

APPENDIX C:
ROLLOUT REFLECTION GUIDE

All of the questions included at the end of each chapter are summarized here. Use this reflection guide to facilitate Rollout planning discussions as a leadership team. Work through these questions together to create alignment and develop your unique Rollout approach.

*You can also download a copy at **RolloutBook.com**.*

- **Leadership Team Sessions**: Work through 1–2 chapters at a time as a team.

- **Individual Preparation**: Have each leader review questions before team discussions.

- **Document Decisions**: Record your answers and revisit them quarterly.

- **Track Progress**: Use these questions to assess Rollout success over time.

- **Stay Flexible**: Adapt questions to fit your unique situation and challenges.

SETTING THE STAGE

CHAPTER 1: THE JOURNEY TO 100 PERCENT STRONG

1. **Human Energy Assessment**: Looking at our current state, is our human energy scattered in different directions, or is it mostly aligned? What would need to change to get everyone "pushing the boulder" in the same direction?

2. **Tool Readiness**: After completing the Rollout Tracker and Organizational Checkup, what surprised us most about where we are? What gaps feel most urgent to address?

CHAPTER 2: WHAT THE HECK IS ROLLOUT?

1. **Revolutionary Change Mindset**: How comfortable is our organization with the kind of fundamental change that Rollout represents? What past change initiatives can we learn from—both successes and failures?

2. **Journey vs. Event Reality**: How will we remind ourselves to stay patient with the Rollout process? Are we prepared for this to be a journey rather than an event?

3. **Success Visualization**: Looking at the five outcomes of successful Rollout (shared vision, shared language, discipline and focus, clear expectations, healthy team dynamics), which of these would have the biggest impact on our current frustrations?

CHAPTER 3: WHY ROLLOUT IS HARD

1. **Resistance Preparation**: Given our team's personalities and past experiences, what specific types of resistance should we expect during Rollout? Which team members might struggle most with the changes, and why?

2. **Our Own Change Journey**: Reflecting on our own EOS learning experience, what moments did we feel most resistant or overwhelmed? How can understanding our own journey help us be more patient with our team's process?

3. **Mindset Check**: Are we approaching this Rollout from a place of excitement about the possibilities, or anxiety about the challenges? How might our mindset influence how our team receives and responds to the changes?

PREPARATION

CHAPTER 4: GETTING READY FOR ROLLOUT

1. **EOS Foundation Assessment**: Which of our five Foundational Tools (V/TO, The Accountability Chart, Rocks, The Meeting Pulse, Scorecard) feels strongest right now? Which needs the most work before Rollout?

2. **Vision Alignment**: Are we genuinely excited about our vision, or are we just going through the motions? What would it take to move from lukewarm to passionate?

3. **Teaching Readiness**: Are we prepared to teach these tools with authentic enthusiasm? What would help us feel more confident as teachers?

4. **Mindset Check**: Are we approaching this Rollout from a place of abundance and trust, or are we holding back

out of fear? What would it look like to be completely transparent with our team?

5. **Rollout Readiness**: Are we ready to move forward with Rollout now, or do we need to strengthen our foundation first? If we're not quite ready, what specific actions will we take in the next 30-60 days to get there?

CHAPTER 5: PLANNING YOUR ROLLOUT

1. **Define Your Approach and Timeline**: Given our company's size, culture, and complexity, should we roll out by department, by tool, or use a hybrid approach?

2. **Clarify Roles and Responsibilities**: Who in our company would be the best internal Rollout Champion? How can we ensure our leadership team and mid-managers are actively engaged in the process?

3. **Plan Your Communication**: What are the biggest concerns or questions our team members are likely to have about our vision and EOS? How can we address these proactively in our communication plan and build in the repetition people need to truly absorb these concepts?

4. **Keep It Simple and Flexible**: How will we stay open to changing our approach based on what we learn?

CHAPTER 6: INTRODUCING YOUR VISION AND EOS

1. **Leadership Team Involvement**: Is our entire leadership team prepared to introduce the vision and EOS together, or are we relying too heavily on one person? What does each leader need to know and be able to explain confidently?

2. **Mid-Manager preparation**: Have we identified and prepared our mid-managers to champion the Rollout? What specific support do they need to carry the message effectively to their teams?

3. **Context Before Content**: For each foundational tool we'll introduce, have we developed clear talking points that explain WHY it matters before diving into WHAT it is? Where might confusion arise if we skip this step?

4. **Making It Visible**: Beyond the initial announcement, how will we keep the vision and EOS visible in daily work? What visual reminders or creative approaches would resonate with our team?

5. **Repetition Discipline**: How will we ensure the vision gets repeated consistently—not just once, but quarter after quarter? What's our plan for regular State of the Company meetings?

INTEGRATION

CHAPTER 7: ROLLING OUT TO DEPARTMENTS

1. **Departmental Structure and Readiness**: How should we define "departments" for Rollout purposes based on who works together regularly? Which teams are ready to start Level 10 Meetings now, and which need more preparation?

2. **Scorecards and Accountability**: What numbers from our leadership Scorecard could form the foundation of departmental Scorecards? How will we ensure each department has meaningful metrics they can actually influence?

3. **Rollout Approach**: Should we roll out one tool at a time across all departments, implement all tools in one department first, or take a hybrid approach? What factors in our organization should influence this decision?

4. **True Understanding**: How will we check whether our team truly understands the vision and EOS concepts beyond just nodding along? What will we do when we discover gaps in understanding?

CHAPTER 8: BRINGING YOUR VISION TO LIFE

1. **Creating an Intentional Culture**: How consistently do we use our Core Values when we hire, fire, review, reward, and recognize? What specific changes would make them more central to how we operate?

2. **Staying Focused**: What opportunities or initiatives are we currently pursuing that don't align with our Core Focus? What would happen if we stopped them to focus on what matters most?

3. **Making a Big Impact**: Is this goal big and energizing for everyone in the company? Are we making steady progress toward our 10-Year Target?

4. **Attracting Ideal Customers**: What percentage of our marketing efforts specifically target our ideal customer profile versus trying to appeal to everyone? How well can our sales team identify prospects who truly fit?

5. **Differentiating Yourself from the Competition**: Can every customer-facing team member clearly explain our 3 Uniques and provide evidence of how we deliver them consistently?

6. **Creating a Great Customer Experience**: Are we using our Proven Process to set, manage, and deliver on expectations to create an exceptional customer experience? Is our guarantee helping us close business and give our customers peace of mind?

CHAPTER 9: CREATING AN ENVIRONMENT OF ACCOUNTABILITY

1. **Core Processes**: Are we ready to identify, simplify, and document our 6–12 Core Processes using the 3-Step Process Documenter? Once we do that, how will we make sure that our processes are consistently followed by everyone? How much time should we allocate in our Rollout plan for completing these activities?

2. **Measurables (Everyone Has a Number):** Are we ready to clarify individual expectations and ensure everyone has a number they are accountable for keeping on track? How long do we think it will take to reach a point where everyone in the organization has a number?

3. **Letting Go of the Vine**: What specific areas are we holding onto too tightly out of fear, and how is our need for control potentially preventing people from taking true ownership of their results? Are there unresolved GWC issues holding us back?

4. **LMA**: Are we ready to learn about the Five Leadership Practices and Five Management Practices? When should we plan to read How to Be a Great Boss as a leadership team? When will we introduce this content to our mid-managers?

SUSTAINABILITY

CHAPTER 10: RUNNING ON EOS... FOREVER

1. **Honestly Assess Your Current Commitment**: When pressure mounts or when EOS feels inconvenient, does our leadership team double down on the disciplines or make exceptions? What does this tell us about our true commitment level?

2. **Evaluate Your "Followed by All" Reality**: Where in our organization do we see strong EOS discipline, and where do we see people picking and choosing which tools to follow? What specific actions will we take to address the gaps?

3. **Review the Four Disciplines of FBA**: Which of the four disciplines (Train, Measure, Manage, Update) is strongest in our organization? Which needs the most attention? What's our plan to strengthen the weakest area?

4. **Make Your Commitment Clear**: What would our organization look like if everyone followed EOS consistently? Are we truly committed to getting EOS followed by all... forever?

APPENDIX D:
ROLLOUT TROUBLESHOOTING GUIDE

The significant problems we face cannot be solved at the same level of thinking we were at when we created them.

—Albert Einstein

No Rollout goes perfectly. Even with careful preparation, clear communication, and strong leadership commitment, you'll hit bumps that test your resolve and require some creative problem-solving. This troubleshooting guide covers the most common Rollout challenges we've seen across hundreds of implementations, along with ideas for getting things back on track.

Running into these issues doesn't mean your Rollout is broken; it means you're human. Every successful EOS organization has faced similar obstacles and found ways to overcome them.

ISSUE #1: PEOPLE KEEP SAYING THEY DON'T HAVE TIME FOR EOS

COMMON SYMPTOMS

- Skipping or showing up late to Level 10 Meetings
- Not preparing for meetings or treating EOS activities as "extra work"
- Complaining about "more meetings" when departments start Level 10 Meetings
- Rock completion rates consistently below 80 percent
- People asking to "just get an update" instead of attending meetings

POSSIBLE ROOT CAUSES

- **Seeing EOS as a Program, Not an Operating System**: People see EOS as additional work rather than a better way of working
- **Poor Prioritization**: Leadership hasn't made it clear that EOS disciplines aren't optional
- **Genuine Overload**: Teams really are swamped and need help with capacity
- **Old Habits Die Hard**: People default to reactive, crisis-driven work instead of planning ahead

THINGS TO TRY

- Have honest conversations about EOS being non-negotiable (not mean, just clear)

- Take a hard look at what people are actually spending time on and eliminate the stuff that doesn't matter
- Share real examples of time saved through better alignment—make the ROI visible
- Do a "Stop Doing" exercise to cut activities that don't align with your Core Focus
- Help managers learn to protect their team's time and say no to distractions
- Face the music on Right People Right Seats issues with chronic resisters

ISSUE #2: LEVEL 10 MEETINGS FEEL FORCED, BORING, OR UNPRODUCTIVE

COMMON SYMPTOMS

- Meeting ratings consistently below 8/10
- People checking phones or zoning out during meetings
- Off-Track Scorecard Measurables that nobody talks about
- IDS sessions that spin in circles without solving anything
- To-dos that never get done
- Same issues showing up week after week
- People showing up unprepared or leaving early

POSSIBLE ROOT CAUSES

- **Weak Facilitation**: Meeting leaders don't know how to keep things moving and focused
- **Wrong Issues**: People bring updates or complaints instead of real problems to solve

- **Meaningless Numbers**: Scorecard metrics that don't actually drive decisions
- **Leader/Manager Not Bought In**: If leaders aren't taking it seriously, nobody else will

THINGS TO TRY

- Get some facilitation training for meeting leaders (it's a skill, not magic)
- Fix your Scorecard so the numbers actually matter and spark conversation
- Practice IDS until it feels natural—it's awkward at first but gets better
- Set ground rules: phones away, laptops closed, everyone engaged
- Show examples of "good issues" vs. "bad issues," so people bring the right stuff
- Try different facilitators to find who's naturally good at it

ISSUE #3: ROCKS CONSISTENTLY DON'T GET COMPLETED

COMMON SYMPTOMS

- Rock completion rates below 70 percent quarter after quarter
- Rocks reported "on track" until suddenly they're "not done"
- Vague or unmeasurable Rocks that nobody can objectively complete
- Last-minute scrambling to show "progress"
- Lots of blaming external circumstances

POSSIBLE ROOT CAUSES

- **Lousy Rock Setting**: Rocks aren't S.M.A.R.T., or aren't actually the most important work
- **Too Much on the Plate**: People are trying to do more than humanly possible
- **No Real Consequences**: Nothing happens when Rocks don't get done
- **Missing Resources**: People don't have the authority, budget, or support they need
- **Poor Planning**: The Rock owner isn't setting aside time, scheduling meetings, or thinking about dependencies that could get in the way of Rock completion

THINGS TO TRY

- Check if current Rocks actually meet S.M.A.R.T. criteria—make sure everyone agrees on what "done" looks like
- Be brutally honest about capacity and cut Rock loads if needed
- Check in on Rocks weekly and jump on problems early
- Use IDS immediately when Rocks go off track instead of hoping they'll fix themselves
- Get better at Rock setting during quarterly planning
- Create real accountability for Rock completion (not punishment, just consequences)
- Help Rock owners learn basic project management skills and tools to plan effectively

ISSUE #4: MID-MANAGERS SEEM RESISTANT OR DISENGAGED

COMMON SYMPTOMS

- Departmental Level 10 Meetings aren't happening regularly
- Managers making excuses for why "EOS won't work" in their area
- Employees confused about expectations or priorities
- The crucial link between leadership and frontline people isn't working

POSSIBLE ROOT CAUSES

- **Skepticism**: Managers think EOS will fizzle out like other past initiatives
- **Skill Gaps**: They don't feel confident teaching EOS to their teams
- **Caught in the Middle**: Stuck between old ways and new expectations
- **Left Out**: They weren't included in Rollout planning and feel like it's being done to them

THINGS TO TRY

- Sit down one-on-one and really listen to their concerns
- Give extra training and support to managers who need it
- Make it clear that EOS makes their job easier, not harder

- Let managers have a say in how EOS gets rolled out in their areas
- Create a manager's group for Rollout feedback and problem-solving

ISSUE #5: DIFFERENT DEPARTMENTS ARE IMPLEMENTING EOS INCONSISTENTLY

COMMON SYMPTOMS

- Some teams crushing Level 10 Meetings while others barely show up
- Different EOS language and approaches across departments
- Wildly different Rock completion and Scorecard discipline
- Employees confused about what's expected company-wide
- Cross-department projects getting messy due to different approaches

POSSIBLE ROOT CAUSES

- **Inconsistent Leadership**: Department heads have different levels of commitment
- **Cultural Differences**: Departments have their own established ways of doing things
- **Uneven Support**: Some departments getting more help and training
- **Unclear Standards**: Nobody's defined what "good enough" looks like across the company

THINGS TO TRY

- Set minimum standards for EOS across all departments (and stick to them)
- Figure out which departments are struggling and why
- Redistribute support to the teams that need it most
- Get departments sharing what's working with each other
- Set up mentoring between strong and struggling departments
- Make training and onboarding consistent everywhere

ISSUE #6: PEOPLE DON'T UNDERSTAND OR REMEMBER THE VISION

COMMON SYMPTOMS

- Team members can't explain Core Values, Core Focus, or other V/TO pieces
- They nod during presentations but can't connect vision to their daily work
- People can't give examples of living the values
- Decisions don't seem to reflect vision alignment

POSSIBLE ROOT CAUSES

- **Information Overload**: Trying to share too much vision content too fast
- **Not Enough Repetition**: Vision shared once or twice instead of constantly

- **Too Abstract**: Talking concepts instead of practical examples
- **No Connection**: People can't see how vision relates to what they actually do

THINGS TO TRY

- Slow down and focus on one V/TO piece at a time
- Give real examples of how vision shows up in everyday work
- Have regular "vision check" conversations to see what's sticking
- Connect vision to current projects and decisions people are making
- Help departments figure out what company vision means for their specific work
- Train managers to weave vision into normal conversations

ISSUE #7: SCORECARDS AREN'T DRIVING THE RIGHT CONVERSATIONS OR ACTIONS

COMMON SYMPTOMS

- Teams track numbers religiously, but Scorecard reviews feel like going through the motions
- Numbers get reported without discussion or analysis
- Off-track numbers don't lead to problem-solving
- People can't explain what drives their numbers

POSSIBLE ROOT CAUSES

- **Wrong Numbers**: Tracking "nice to know" stuff instead of "need to know" indicators
- **Too Many Numbers**: If everything is important, nothing is important
- **No Clear Targets**: Numbers without goals don't create accountability
- **Bad Data**: Inaccurate or missing information makes discussions pointless
- **No Action Focus**: Teams report numbers but don't talk about what to do

THINGS TO TRY

- Ask about each number: "Does this actually drive decisions or actions?"
- Set clear goals for every number so people know what "on track" means
- Fix data collection so numbers are accurate and timely
- Train people to ask "Why?" when numbers are off and "What are we going to do?"
- Get rid of numbers that never spark conversation
- Add leading indicators that help predict problems before they hit

ISSUE #8: INITIAL ENTHUSIASM HAS FADED, AND OLD HABITS ARE RETURNING

COMMON SYMPTOMS

- The launch excitement has worn off, and people are sliding back to old ways
- Level 10 Meetings getting skipped, Rock discipline getting sloppy
- Vision talk disappearing from daily conversations
- Meeting attendance and engagement declining
- People stop using EOS language when it's not required

POSSIBLE ROOT CAUSES

- **Change Fatigue**: People naturally resist sustained behavior change—it's biology
- **Not Seeing Results**: Teams haven't experienced enough wins to keep them motivated
- **Leadership Slipping**: Leaders skip EOS disciplines, sending the wrong message
- **Lack of Reinforcement**: Old habits are easier and more comfortable

THINGS TO TRY

- Leadership team needs to publicly recommit and model the behavior
- Find and celebrate specific wins that came from EOS—make success visible

- Address the slide directly with individuals and teams
- Remind people why you're doing this and what's at stake
- Make EOS adherence visible and expected, not just hoped for
- Create success stories that highlight real benefits people are experiencing

ISSUE #9: NEW HIRES AREN'T INTEGRATING WELL INTO THE EOS CULTURE

COMMON SYMPTOMS

- New people struggling to understand expectations or participate in meetings
- They seem confused by EOS terminology or resistant to the structure
- New hires can't explain basic EOS concepts after 4–6 weeks
- They're passive in Level 10 Meetings or not participating well

POSSIBLE ROOT CAUSES

- **Weak Onboarding**: EOS isn't built into new hire orientation
- **Culture Shock**: New employees come from less structured places
- **No Support System**: Nobody's helping them learn EOS tools and expectations

- **Hiring Mismatch**: Recruiting process doesn't check for EOS compatibility

THINGS TO TRY

- Build comprehensive EOS orientation into the first week for every new hire
- Assign EOS mentors to guide new people through their first quarter
- Give them *What the Heck is EOS?* and other learning resources
- Set up 30/60/90 day check-ins specifically about vision and EOS integration
- Pair new hires with people who love EOS for peer learning

ISSUE #10: NEW LEADERS ARE UNDERMINING EOS DISCIPLINE

COMMON SYMPTOMS

- New managers suggesting "better" meeting formats they used at previous companies
- Implementation of complex management systems that bypass Rock discipline
- Creation of reporting structures that conflict with your Accountability Chart
- Comments like "This is too basic" or "We don't need all this structure"

- Teams becoming confused about which systems to follow
- EOS tools and disciplines are "drifting" or being abandoned
- Employees questioning whether the organization is still committed to EOS

POSSIBLE ROOT CAUSES

- **Pressure to Prove Value**: New leaders feel they need to show immediate impact by introducing familiar methods
- **EOS Learning Curve**: Learning new systems feels uncomfortable for accomplished professionals who are used to being experts
- **Competing Methodologies**: They bring impressive toolboxes full of systems that conflict with EOS
- **Inadequate Onboarding**: EOS expectations weren't made clear during hiring or orientation
- **Cultural Misunderstanding**: They don't realize that undermining EOS threatens the foundation of organizational success

THINGS TO TRY

- Make it crystal clear during interviews that your organization runs on EOS, and all leaders must embrace these tools
- Pair new leaders with successful EOS champions who can guide them
- When new leaders suggest alternatives or try to implement competing systems, have direct conversations about expectations

- Explain that while their experience is valuable, organizational success comes from everyone following the same system
- Give them *What the Heck is EOS?* and other materials to deepen understanding

REMEMBER

You didn't hire them to change your operating system; you hired them to excel within it. The strength of your EOS implementation depends on everyone, especially leaders, consistently following the same system. Don't let new talent dilute the discipline that created your success in the first place.

GENERAL TROUBLESHOOTING IDEAS

When you hit any Rollout challenge, keep these things in mind:

1. **Figure Out the Root Issue**. Don't jump to solutions. Ask "Why is this really happening?" before deciding what to do about it.
2. **People Issues Usually Come First.** Most EOS problems are people problems wearing disguises. If someone consistently struggles, figure out if it's training, capacity, or a Right Person Right Seat issue.
3. **Look at Leadership First.** If EOS isn't working at lower levels of the organization, check what the leadership team is modeling. People copy what they see, not what they hear.
4. **Progress Over Perfection.** Small, steady improvements are better than dramatic changes that don't stick. Celebrate progress while keeping standards.

5. **Be Patient but Persistent.** Real change takes time, but it also needs consistent reinforcement. Don't give up too fast, but don't accept chronic non-performance either.

6. **Use EOS to Fix EOS Problems.** When facing EOS challenges, use EOS to solve them. Drop issues down, use IDS, and create To-dos with clear ownership.

7. **Remember Why You Started.** When Rollout gets tough, reconnect with your vision and why you started this journey. The benefits are worth the effort.

DON'T BE AFRAID TO ASK FOR HELP

Sometimes you need an outside perspective. Consider getting support from your Professional EOS Implementer, or from the wider community of companies running on EOS when:

- Multiple issues keep happening despite your best efforts
- Leadership team alignment breaks down around EOS
- Results stay disappointing, even though you're using the tools
- Resistance becomes widespread and entrenched
- You want objective assessment and specific recommendations

Getting help isn't giving up; it's being smart about success. Every organization successfully running on EOS has faced these challenges and worked through them. The key is staying committed to getting EOS followed by all, while learning and adapting as you go.

Your Rollout isn't failing because you hit problems; it's succeeding because you're committed to solving them. Keep going, keep learning, and keep trusting the process.

The vision you've created is worth the effort it takes to get there.

ENDNOTES

1. Gino Wickman, *Traction: Get A Grip on Your Business* (Dallas, TX: BenBella Books, 2011), 17.
2. Thomas Gordon, *Parent Effectiveness Training: The Proven Program for Raising Responsible Children* (New York, NY: Harmony Books, 2019).
3. Wickman, *Traction*.
4. Gino Wickman and Tom Bouwer, *What the Heck Is EOS?: A Complete Guide for Employees in Companies Running on EOS* (Dallas, TX: BenBella Books, Inc, 2017).
5. Wickman, *Traction*.
6. Wickman, *Traction*.

ACKNOWLEDGMENTS

Writing a book is never a solo endeavor, even when there are two of us. This book came to life because of the support, wisdom, and generosity of countless people who believed in this work and in us.

We cooked up the idea for this book poolside in San Antonio after the EOS Implementer Annual Meeting, convinced we'd captured something essential about helping leadership teams roll out EOS to their entire organizations. Everyone thought we were crazy to take this on—and we were! But through countless Zoom calls, Marco Polos, texts, and emails squeezed between client sessions, we made it happen. We learned a lot, deepened our mastery, and strengthened our friendship along the way. It wasn't quite as fun as singing in a choir, but we still made beautiful music together!

To **Gino Wickman**: Thank you for creating a system that has profoundly changed our lives and those of hundreds of thousands of entrepreneurs around the world – and for trusting us with the material you so lovingly created. Your review of our draft and the philosophical context you provided helped us ensure we honored the integrity of EOS while addressing the critical challenge of company-wide rollout.

To **Jill Young**, our "book doula": We can't thank you enough for imparting your magic and wisdom on us during the developmental stages of this book. That brainstorming session in Ann Arbor helped us transform a loose collection of ideas into a coherent framework. You helped us find our voice and our structure.

To the **Wise Women Community**: Your support, encouragement, and wisdom sustained us through the inevitable doubts and challenges of bringing this book to life.

To our fellow **EOS Implementers** and **test readers** who reviewed drafts and provided invaluable feedback: Mike Gruley, Jeremy Lopatin, Elizabeth Davis, Sonja Jury, Rene Boer, Drew Spurgers, Alice Jordan, Haraya Del Rosario Gust, Victoria Cabot, Lisa Gonzalez, Anastasia Toomey, Gavin Brauer, Rick Wilson, Anik Ganguly, Dan Hirst, Scott Longfellow, and Beth Berman. Your insights from the field made this book richer, more practical, and more real.

To **Kelly Knight** and **Mark O'Donnell** at EOS Worldwide: Thank you for your support of this project. And to **Amber Baird**, **Victoria Cabot**, **Roxanne Ntagazwa**, **Akisha Burgett**, and **Jennifer Yruegas**: Thank you for helping us navigate the orange tape with patience and good humor.

To the team at **Igniting Souls**—**Teri Kojetin**, **Tanisha Williams**, **Sarah Grandstaff**, and **Jill Ellis**: Thank you for believing in this book and for guiding us through the publishing process with expertise and care.

To **Drew Robinson** and **Spork Design**: Your artful illustrations brought clarity and visual interest to complex concepts. Thank you for making this book not just useful, but beautiful.

To the team at **Wayne Media**: Thank you for partnering with us to bring this book to life beyond the page—through our website, podcasts, video, social channels, and every piece of collateral. You made our book vision visible.

To the **leaders and companies** who allowed us to share their stories: Total Security Solutions, Meadowlark Builders, Güd Marketing, Konrady Plastics, Professional Benefits Administrators, HOH Water Technologies, Global Parts & Maintenance, Campus Cooks, Silverlake Design & Marketing,

Four Seasons Kanga Roof, Skidmore Sales and Distributing Co, Clear Height Properties, City of Faith, CG Financial, Blue Chip Partners, and LeadingIT. Your vulnerability in sharing both your failures and successes makes this book real. We hope we've honored your trust by presenting your journeys in ways that will help others avoid the same pitfalls and embrace the same breakthroughs.

To **all of our EOS clients**: You are the reason this book exists. Every principle, every tool, every insight came from watching you navigate the messy, beautiful work of getting your entire organization running on EOS. Thank you for the privilege of being part of your transformations.

FROM MARISA

To my kids, **Charlotte and Caitlin**: Thank you for understanding when I disappeared into my office for yet another writing session, and for pretending to be interested when I talked about the book during our weekly family breakfasts at Zingerman's Roadhouse.

To my mom, **Dolly**: Thank you for providing much of the psychological and brain science context for the chapter on Why Rollout Is Hard. Your expertise helped ground our practical experience in solid research.

To my dad, **Dale**: Thank you for teaching me how to edit and simplify, and how to keep vast amounts of information organized and categorized. Those skills made this book possible.

To **Dozer Coffee**: Thank you for fueling me with brown-sugar lattes and blueberry muffins throughout countless writing sessions. You kept me caffeinated and happy.

To my friends **Liz**, **Kristin**, and **Holly**: Thank you for your support on the emotional rollercoaster that is writing a book. You listened, encouraged, and reminded me why this mattered.

To my first EOS client, **Jim Richards**: Thank you for believing in me ten years ago and for always challenging me to raise the bar. You set the standard for what great clients look like.

To **Don Tinney**, co-founder of EOS Worldwide, and **Mike Kotsis**: Thank you for the opportunity to join the EOS Worldwide leadership team and for encouraging me to become an EOS Implementer. You helped me see possibilities I couldn't see for myself.

To **Jeremy Lopatin**, **Mike Gruley, and the Michigan EOS Implementer Community**: Thank you for being my biggest cheerleaders and for being a sounding board for book ideas. Your enthusiasm and wise counsel kept me going when the work felt overwhelming.

FROM BETH

To my husband, **Mike**, and my kids, **Aidan**, **Erin**, and **Liam**: Thank you for your patience with the weekend writing sessions, the distracted dinners, and all the times I said, "Just one more chapter." Your support and belief in me made this possible.

To my dad, **Rob**: Thank you for teaching me the importance of data and for showing me what being a great boss really looks like—those lessons shaped not just this book, but my entire approach to leadership.

To my mom, **Kate**: Although you're not with us anymore, your love of language and great storytelling lives within me.

To **Rene Boer**: Thank you for the opportunity to partner with you on Great Boss Workshops and for providing me with a deep understanding of the human side of LMA. That partnership transformed how I see leadership development.

To **Jim Coyle**: Your early belief in me was the essential fuel I needed, seeing potential I hadn't yet recognized. Thank you for your continued coaching, which has profoundly shaped my entire EOS journey.

To the **Chicago EOS Implementer Community**: Thank you for your support and enthusiasm. Being part of this community reminds me every day why I love this work.

—ɯ—

This book represents thousands of hours of client work, hundreds of conversations with fellow Implementers, and the wisdom of leaders who were brave enough to try something challenging. If it helps even one leadership team successfully roll out EOS to their entire organization, every moment will have been worth it.

ABOUT THE AUTHORS

Marisa Smith has always been fascinated by how great businesses work. That curiosity turned into a career of helping leaders build stronger, healthier companies.

In 2002, she founded a marketing and consulting agency that grew to serve clients across the country. Like many entrepreneurs, she eventually hit a ceiling and realized she needed a better system to grow. When she discovered the Entrepreneurial Operating System, it completely changed how she operated and allowed her to step out of day-to-day management.

That experience led her to join the leadership team at EOS Worldwide, where she led a marketing strategy that helped the company grow by more than 400 percent. Seeing what EOS could do for others inspired her to become an Expert EOS Implementer and dedicate her work to helping leadership teams gain clarity, accountability, and traction.

Today, she coaches and facilitates EOS sessions in Ann Arbor, Michigan, helping business owners simplify how they run their companies and get back to loving what they do.

—ᴍᴍ—

Beth Fahey has sat in just about every seat a leader can. From entrepreneur to overwhelmed manager to president of a national trade group. She's worked in film, built a bakery from the ground up, and led teams through the kind of real-world challenges you can't learn from a book.

That lived experience is exactly what she brings to the table as an Expert EOS Implementer and leadership coach. Beth helps business owners and leadership teams get clear on what they want, build accountability, and create the kind of company people actually want to be part of.

Beth co-created the "Great Boss Workshops" with René Boer, a practical program that helps managers become leaders their teams truly deserve. She also hosts the Bad Boss Confessional podcast, sharing authentic stories about leadership—mistakes, lessons, and growth.

Beth brings a grounded, creative perspective to EOS implementation, believing it's fundamentally about people, growth, and navigating change with intention. Based in the Chicago area, she's passionate about helping leaders become their best selves in business and life.

Ready To Put What You've Learned Into Action?

Your Rollout Toolkit Awaits

Visit Rolloutbook.com to download free tools and resources:

- **Rollout Tracker** – Monitor your progress through all four phases of rollout

- **Rollout Reflection Guide** - Use this comprehensive planning tool to guide your Rollout journey.

- **Rollout Troubleshooting Guide** – Get solutions for the 10 most common rollout challenges

    ....and more!

These practical tools will help you move from planning to execution—and keep your rollout on track quarter after quarter.

VISIT ROLLOUTBOOK.COM TO ACCESS YOUR FREE RESOURCES TODAY.

Connect with
MARISA
Smith

Achieve Your Vision With EOS®

MARISA-SMITH.COM

Connect with
Beth Fahey

Learn to Lead with Purpose

BethFahey.com

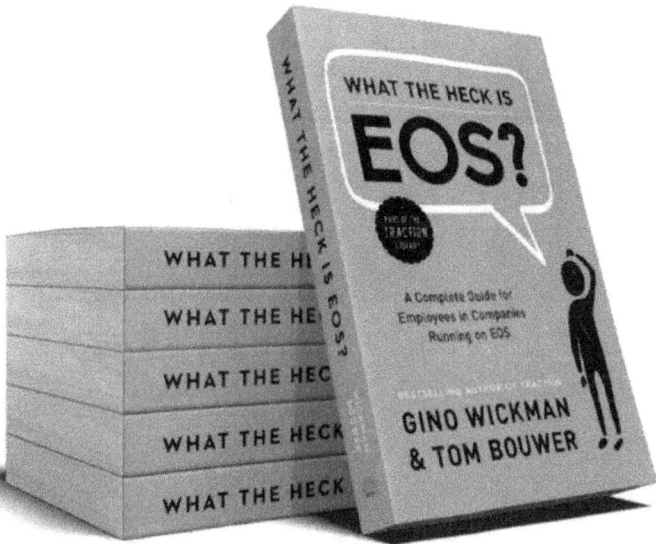

EOS®

ENTREPRENEURIAL
OPERATING SYSTEM®

GET A GRIP ON
YOUR BUSINESS

WITH THE
ENTREPRENEURIAL
OPERATING SYSTEM®

EOSWorldWide.com